# STOP NEGOTIATING WITH YOUR TEEN

◼

Strategies for Parenting
Your Angry, Manipulative, Moody, or
Depressed Adolescent

Janet Sasson Edgette, Psy.D., M.P.H.

*A Perigee Book*

A Perigee Book
Published by The Berkley Publishing Group
A division of Penguin Putnam Inc.
375 Hudson Street
New York, New York 10014

First edition: August 2002

Visit our website at www.penguinputnam.com

Library of Congress Cataloging-in-Publication Data

Edgette, Janet Sasson.
Stop negotiating with your teen : strategies for parenting your angry, manipulative, moody, or depressed adolescent / Janet Sasson Edgette.—1st ed.
p. cm.
ISBN 0-399-52789-3
1. Parent and teenager. 2. Adolescent psychology. 3. Parenting. I. Title.
HQ799.15 .E34 2002
649'.125—dc21          2002025119

Printed in the United States of America

10  9

**"Do not go the way fear bids you to go."**

Jalal ad-Din ar-Rumi, Persian poet

# DEDICATION

*From its inception, this book has been dedicated*
*to my mother, Sarah Sasson—enigmatic, impish, resolute.*
*Too soon afterward, the dedication would be to her memory.*
*How I cherished her. How I miss her.*

# TABLE OF CONTENTS

SECTION TWO:
*Family Stories*

*Conclusion*

# ACKNOWLEDGMENTS

I wish to thank my teachers of the trade, my psychology and psychotherapy professors at Hahnemann University in Philadelphia. Thank you also to my dear father, whose dignity and compassionate doctoring gave me my most vivid model for doctoring compassionately myself. Thank you also to Kevin Lang of The Bedford Book Works, Inc., and Sheila Curry Oakes, Executive Editor of Perigee Books. Thank you to Jane D. Dystel, President of Jane Dystel Literary Management, Inc., for her welcome and support. And thank you many times over to my gem of a husband, John, who bears the brunt of my ambitions, and who has taught me the most about what it means to simultaneously be kind, fair, and dignified in the face of unnerving confoundment.

# INTRODUCTION

There are teenagers who, as expected during their adolescence, push the envelope with their parents and cause their fair share of family strain and exasperation. They insist on more independence than they can handle, test limits, and mess up. But in the end, no one is too worse off for the wear. The kid launches satisfactorily into young adulthood, and the parents breathe a sigh of relief.

Then there are other teenagers. These kids push the envelope and don't stop pushing until their parents throw up their hands. They assume privileges and dispensations. They feel entitled to burden family members with their demands or chronic irritability or bad tempers. They wreak havoc with family life and never hold themselves accountable for the trail of weariness, frustration, worry, or sadness left in the wake of their behaviors. They are not well equipped for young adulthood and launch into it poorly. They often become more dependent on their parents to function than they can stand to acknowledge and direct their self-contempt toward their parents.

This book was written for the parents of that second type of teenager. These are the parents who come into my psychology practice wondering how they can help their child become a more responsible, thoughtful, *likeable* person. They feel bullied by their teenager's rationalizations and manipulated by their moodiness or the omnipresent threat of emotional rages. They know their kids are smart, but they see them making poor choices. They know they are unhappy, but they don't understand why. They know their kids need help, but they don't know how to help them. They cannot easily influence, affect, or persuade their son or daughter, and, rightfully, this frightens them.

I wrote *Stop Negotiating with Your Teen* from more than fifteen years of experience working as a psychologist with all types of children and adolescents and their families. It reflects my belief that good parenting is not about power and control, but about dignity and connection. Parents need to be asking more from their children and teenagers in terms of participating as family and community members, but they also need to be emotionally accessible, warm, forgiving, and forthright with their children. This book teaches parents how to balance the tenuous scales of limit-setting and flexibility, candor and discretion, and compassion and accountability. It also teaches parents how to stand firm in the face of their teenager's persuasions, arguments, or tantrums and hold them accountable for their choices in spite of the teen's attempts to view his or her problems as somebody else's fault.

Practical, contemporary, and filled with colorful examples from my practice, *Stop Negotiating with Your Teen* is designed to help parents find ways to reassert their authority within the household without becoming authoritarian and regain—or develop for the first time—the ability to positively influence their teenage children through words and actions that don't beseech, condemn, or implore, but rather assert, engage, and inspire.

Janet Sasson Edgette
Chester Springs, Pennsylvania
December 2001

# SECTION ONE

◼

# *Regaining Influence over the Difficult Teenage Child*

# 1

## HOW TEENAGERS NEUTRALIZE THEIR PARENTS' AUTHORITY

*Sixteen-year-old Julie has been holding her parents hostage for months with her sullen silence, withdrawal, and sarcastic outbursts. Fearful of "making things worse" or of "upsetting Julie even more," Marie and Nathan have become nearly paralyzed with self-consciousness in their efforts to manage and talk to her—their own daughter!*

*"If we try to ask her what's wrong, she snaps our heads off or storms up to her room. If we try and just make easy conversation, like 'How's school?' she looks at us as if we're idiots. And forget it if we try to tell her what to do or what time to be home! She'll start screaming that we don't trust her and that we're the cause of all her problems. And she won't even tell us what those problems are. She seems so miserable. All we want to do is help. . . ."*

Day after day in contemporary America, this is a common scenario. A teenager wrestles silently with anger, depression, or some other problem while her parents, alienated and bewildered, try to intervene. They speak and behave so carefully, not intending to offend their child, but their careful approach only further fuels the teenager's disdain. So the cycle begins again: The parents try harder to make contact, and the teen pulls farther away.

Marie and Nathan are two of countless devoted, well-meaning parents similarly surprised to find themselves working so hard to make emotional contact with their enigmatic adolescent while simultaneously trying to avoid conflict in the process. These parents mince words, beat around the bush, tolerate discourtesies, make excuses, allow themselves to be ignored, and otherwise neglect to hold their teen accountable for his or her choices, attitudes, or behaviors, which in anyone's book would be considered inappropriate, inconsiderate, or even rude. In some families, the situation has deteriorated to a point that the parents find themselves inactivated or nearly silenced by the threat of their teenager's moodiness, tantrums, argumentativeness, or violence. Parents don't want the hassle; aren't sure what to say anymore; have come to doubt themselves; or are maybe just too tired, too frustrated, or too overwhelmed. They know they should act, but they choose not to. Many never come to realize that the periodic conflicts and drawn-out silent wars averted by their leniencies create a bigger problem by indulging the teenager. In the end, everybody loses.

Responsibility for this unfortunate situation must be shared among the adolescents themselves, their parents, their educators, society, and the media. Typical adolescent defiance finds a perfect foil in the libertarian nature of our society and its institutions of family and education. Parents want to raise self-confident, independent children who can identify and ask for what they want, but they often fall prey to their teen's demands for a voice, rights, and freedom of choice by not balancing these freedoms with accountability. More and more, educators are urged by their administrations to accommodate to the student who *won't* learn, as opposed to the one who *can't.* These educators are forced to tolerate disdain from someone thirty years their junior who knows that Mom or Dad will protect him from his forgetfulness and impudence. The media reports countless tragedies of violence in terms of perpetrators' actions, never remarking on or analyzing these actions as *choices,* underscoring a perception of blamelessness. Moreover, American society historically has tended to indulge the *concept* of adolescence by romanticizing misadventures and improprieties as "stuff teenagers do." As a consequence, millions of teenagers have adopted attitudes of entitlement, manifesting in a generation of kids, many of whom largely expect to be able to do and speak as they please.

Perhaps nowhere are the consequences of this seen more poignantly than in the home. Irresolute parents and self-entitled teenagers stop talking with one another in genuine, authentic ways, and conversations become increasingly superficial, censored, and devoid of emotions. Relationships grow distant or, worse, estranged.

I hear parents say, "I love my child, but I'm not enjoying him very much right now." They are saddened and frustrated by the remote quality of their relationships with their teenage sons and daughters but have resigned themselves to not interacting with their kids as long as it keeps the peace. I explain that overlooking or trying to tiptoe around problems in the relationship or in the teenager's behavior in the hope of avoiding escalating the tension is a mistake. In fact, the more tentative parents become around their teenagers, and the more they try to gain a connection through soliciting their humor or approval, the worse the relationship *and* the teenager's behavior become. When parents abdicate authority and power, rather than making the teenager more receptive to the parent's preferences, the teen feels even more out of control and angry. The parents, then, feel increasingly ineffectual and helpless. The teen and the parents scurry back to their private, silent corners, and the problems are never addressed.

THAT'S what happened in Noah's family. Noah ruled the roost at home with his surly temperament and mean, vocal outbursts. He procrastinated impossibly about house chores and ignored his curfew.

"Noah, you need to clean up after your lunch."

"I'm too tired to do it now. I'll do it later."

"Noah, 'later' never seems to happen," says Dad.

"I'm too tired! " came Noah's reply. "I said I'll do it later. I have to go upstairs anyway and call someone."

"Noah," Dad says weakly, as his son skips up the stairs to his room and telephone, "I really need you to be more responsible around here. . . ."

"Oh, just let it go, Carl," sighs Grace, Noah's mom. "I really want to have a peaceful afternoon, and with Mom and Pop coming over later, well, you know what it will be like if he's angry and everything. He'll make all of us miserable. It's just not worth it."

Noah's parents felt obligated to tolerate their son's moodiness to save their day from misery, so they decided to let this incident slide. It seemed innocuous, after all—just a couple of lunch dishes. It wasn't worth the price of a pleasant afternoon.

Here is where Noah's parents (and many other parents) make a seemingly small allowance that has enormous repercussions. By their not insisting Noah do his chores, he was learning that he didn't need to take his parents' requests seriously. He had discovered that *he* could decide when he would abide their requests and fulfill his responsibilities and when he wouldn't. This was a lesson with pervasive ramifications, because you can be sure that Noah's casual dismissal of his parents wasn't going to stop with the dishes. If Noah's parents allowed this to continue it would spread to everything—his handling of other chores around the house, his homework, his level of engagement with the family, and his attitudes toward family members. It would be carried over to his handling of responsibilities and relationships outside the home as well. Noah needed his parents to be as firm about the dishes, *or, more correctly, about his dismissive attitude toward their multiple requests to do the dishes,* as they might have been about other matters that could be considered "more important"—school assignments, rules about driving, or protocols for having friends over.

The most important thing that Noah's parents could teach him in this situation was an understanding that his treating the relationship between himself and his parents as if it was one among peers was inappropriate and unacceptable. Noah's grasping this would serve as a foundation for his future relations with other adults such as teachers, coaches, supervisors, officials, and employers. In addition, it would foster a self-respect that comes from comfortably accepting a junior status without feeling as if it's an affront to one's dignity or autonomy.

"Well, at least he's not on drugs or something," is a popular excuse made by parents wanting to circumvent skirmishes over "little things." Drugs certainly are worse than a sinkful of crusty dishes, but the issue of respecting one's self and those with whom you live, work, and play are as relevant in one situation as they are in any other. Eventually, the issue becomes not whether or not the dishes are getting done or how many friends are too many to have over without a parent around, but a question of *What is my kid learning about being a responsible member of society and about living flexibly and respectfully with other people?*

Noah's parents chose to let the matter of the dishes slide because they wanted to "protect" the afternoon visit by Noah's grandparents. In doing so, they missed an opportunity to address a more pressing issue—Noah's belief, apparent in how he spoke to his parents, that he was *entitled to make his own, unilateral decisions* regarding house rules. Parents often fail to recognize the underpinnings of the interactions with their children, instead addressing the more obvious behavioral infraction: *"Put the dishes away now!"* rather than, *"You speak to your mom and I as if we were your roommates, all keeping house together. We're not, so start washing."*

## Meta-Communication

This is the "meta"-communication, a commentary about the *way* something is expressed or experienced—in this case,

Noah's behavior and manner of speaking to his parents—rather than about the *result* of an act or *content* of a remark. Meta-communication allows parents to get beyond the trappings of many arguments that, on the surface, appear to be about taking out the trash, or getting good enough grades, or acting appropriately at the breakfast table, and into the *real* issues (typically, entitlement or lack of awareness and respect) that keep the spurious bickering alive and kicking.

Take, for instance, Kate, who marches angrily around the house demanding a less restrictive curfew. Her insistence that she wouldn't be so morose and sarcastic if only her parents would let her stay out later with her friends, and her parents' responding as though the issue was literally about curfews, robs all of them of the *opportunity to address Kate's assumption that it is okay to express displeasure by imposing it on those believed to be responsible,* rather than finding more mature and direct ways to deal with the problem.

While Noah's parents worry that Noah might respond to firm limit-setting by starting his engines for a verbal row, they need to learn to press on in spite of the unpleasant short-term consequences for the sake of bringing about enduring change in the way their son handles frustration. If Noah is still ranting and raving when Grandmom and Grandpop come to visit, he will be asked to excuse himself and have his fit elsewhere. If he speaks rudely, he will be asked to apologize, and if he refuses to do this, he will be informed of which privilege he has just lost. If he is sullen and pouty, he will be ignored. *If Noah's parents let their son's reaction to being held accountable for his earlier decisions about the dishes play havoc with the afternoon visit, it would be an enormous mistake and serve to*

9

*transfer power to Noah.* He alone is responsible for his reactions and will come to acknowledge that (which he already knows is true but pretends not to) only when the adults around him stop talking to him as if he needs to be convinced.

In such a situation, Carl and Grace could say to their son, "It's unfortunate that you drew such a line in the sand about the dishes, but we're not going to back down just because we don't want Grandmom and Grandpop to see you huffing and puffing around. Decide how you want to handle it." When an adolescent's outbursts begin to disturb his own mood or his own plans more than those of his parents, he will curtail them.

If Grandmom and Grandpop were to challenge Noah's parents and try to hold *them* responsible for their "poor grandson's" mood, Carl and Grace would need to explain Noah's mood in light of what had happened and in light of the changes in their parenting style. They would also need to ask directly for the grandparents' support. Noah's parents could explain that, while in the past they might have tried to appease Noah's anger, they've come to realize that his temper has been too indulged, and he has grown too self-centered. In addition, they might go on to describe Noah's dramatics as an expectable, but hopefully short-lived, attempt to convince the powers that be to return to the old ways. The onus would then be on Grandmom and Grandpop to respect Noah's parents' wishes and management approach.

NO one means to raise a child who acts irresponsibly or ungraciously. And when that child's unbecoming manner becomes apparent, no one is more surprised than his or her parents. Fortunately, the problem is usually remediable. However, it requires that the parents do things in a very different fashion from the way they have been doing them. It is often difficult and frustrating to change, especially for people whose relations are characterized by denial or an avoidance of conflict. Moreover, parents usually assume that it's the kid who is going to have to make changes, not them. Parents are surprised, sometimes dismayed, to discover that it is only when they change their parenting techniques that the child or adolescent begins to relate, behave, react, handle, or think about things differently.

## A Different Approach to Parenting

Some children are more challenging than others to raise, and some parents are more easily intimidated by their child's emotional reactiveness and overly defensive postures than are others. However, the parents who have the least trouble getting their kids to appreciate the values they are trying to impart:

- are confident in their parenting without being authoritarian or severe;

- are clear and consistent in their expectations;

- always treat their children with respect, no matter how angry, disappointed, or frustrated they are; and

- remain verbally and physically demonstrative and affectionate throughout the child's adolescence.

They maintain:

- a sense of humor;

- an emotional accessibility; and

- a balanced perspective, allowing them to accurately designate one problem as important and another as unimportant.

Moreover, they:

- stand their ground on the points that matter; and

- never patronize, demean, or punish unfairly.

These attributes are immeasurably helpful in the face of a teenager who uses contempt, sarcasm, and/or withdrawal in an attempt to get a parent to back down, let up, drop, or otherwise abandon a perfectly good position or standard. The child who uses his heightened emotional reactivity as a way to intimidate a parent rather than to connect and get support is a tougher child to raise. The parents who try to solve this problem by becoming less insistent, thinking that by using a softer approach they'll avoid the quarrels and alienation that threaten amiable family life, are often terribly disappointed to find that the tactic doesn't work. Primarily, it doesn't work because no one can resolve differences by avoiding them. Facing them head-on, however, doesn't mean the parents have signed on to living in a war zone. By being sensitive to the aspect of an adolescent's complaint or concern that is legitimate, and by letting the adolescent know that they remain committed to her welfare and to working things out, moms and dads can usually retain the goodwill of even the most cantankerous and resistant of kids. Extending the olive branch is an entirely different animal from relaxing one's standards, and it's only when parents blur the two, or have trouble being simultaneously forgiving and firm, that efforts to be sensitive and flexible can slip into being too passive or too indulgent.

## Walking on Eggshells with Emotionally Reactive Teenagers Doesn't Work

☐ *Getting parents to back off is exactly what the overly emotional or dramatic adolescent is trying to do in order to escape accountability for her mood, attitude, or behavior.*

One of the first steps in establishing a kind but authoritative power within the home is the parents' recognition that their feelings of acute self-consciousness, self-doubt, or intimidation may be a result of their adolescent's attempts to disarm them. Parents who don't see their teenager's self-righteousness and line-in-the-sand threats as efforts to get the parents to *stop parenting* are at risk for *over*empathizing with their child's distress. Parents must learn to sympathize with their adolescent's genuine grievances and be open to addressing them fairly, but without giving away the farm. When Julie's parents told her that they would tolerate her rejection of their help but not the rude manner in which she rejected it, Julie began to tone down her sarcastic and contemptuous responses to their questions about what troubled her. Noah's parents learned not to give in to his teary requests to stay out later than curfew in order to be with his friends until he demonstrated more responsibility around the house. It was tempting for them to acquiesce because he was beginning to make some friends, and his parents wanted to support these new friendships. However, *it was critical that it never become more important for Noah's parents than for Noah* that he nurse those friendships along and make the necessary changes in his attitude that would allow him to do so.

Seventeen-year-old Ross wasn't tolerating any discussion with his parents about his prospects for summer work. He knew that he needed to have a job in place for the beginning of July, but by the third week of June he'd only applied to a few local businesses. None had called him back. His parents' questions about job prospects or any kind of back-up plan were met with Ross's angry tirades or his storming out of the room.

"Even when we approach him to help, he gets angry," Ross's mom, Debby, told me. Ross's dad nodded vigorously in agreement.

"I asked him just the other day if he would like me to sit down with him and make a list of places he could get applications from," said Nick. "And he started yelling and carrying on that he was already planning on getting more applications and that it wasn't his fault he didn't have a job by now, it was the economy's. But I happen to know that he only applied to three places, and I think two of them weren't even hiring."

"What happens if he doesn't find work by July?" I asked.

"Well, I don't know. I guess we'll have to figure that out," replied Debby. She looked over at Nick, who shrugged.

"If Ross knows, as he probably does, that you guys haven't figured out what happens if he doesn't follow through, he'll likely wait until July to find out along with you."

"You mean you don't think he's really going to find work?" Nick asked.

"From your account of things, there is no reason to believe that your son is earnestly looking. And you're making it easy for him to blow it off by backing down when he blows up."

"It's just that I feel bad for him. He's never been good at jobs, really, even little ones around the house or yard," said Debby. "Last year he got 'fired' by one of our neighbors who had hired him to help with his storage center. He didn't want to let Ross go, but Ross wasn't doing what he needed to. Plus, he wouldn't always show up. Ross wouldn't let us talk to him about it after it happened, and he laid around pretty much the rest of the summer. I just worry that he feels badly about himself, so I hate to keep bringing it up. Besides, when I do, he makes life miserable for the next few days with his stomping around and his silent treatments."

"He has learned how to shut you guys down," I remarked, "and you are paying a miserable price. But so is your son, and he needs you to tell him that and to mobilize him. Tell Ross that his defensiveness about finding and keeping a job are holding the two of you hostage to a lousy bunch of options. Because he's not taking the initiative to bring the subject up, you have to. But when you do, he acts indignant and tries to make you sorry you ever asked. Yet if you don't bring it up, you are left completely in the dark about his progress or his plans. Explain to him that you are available to help him find a job but that he needs to let you know how he wants you to help. Don't continue going to him. Also tell him that the economy notwithstanding, he needs to have found work by July or be able to demonstrate to you serious effort at finding a job, or there will be some consequence. The consequence should be something you decide is appropriate—loss of the car except for interviewing, for example. Ross needs you to sympathize with his difficulties with responsibility and jobs and the like but also to help him make sure his lack of follow-through and other behaviors don't become a problem that haunts him into and throughout his adulthood."

> ▣ *Each time a parent doesn't address a problem that arises, she is whittling away at her credibility as a parent who is committed to teaching her child right from wrong.*

There are practical reasons for letting some problems go, but a pattern of looking past certain problems or undesirable behaviors because they are too small, too infrequent, or too inconsequential spells trouble. Kids are quick to pick up on what is important to their parents, and they understand that matters outside that circle of attention are easily dismissed for lack of time or interest. Despite how fluently a parent rationalizes her dismissal of problems due to busy-ness, fatigue, or libertarian child-rearing philosophies, the child or adolescent whose parent is inconsistent about upholding important social and familial values learns that their value is conditional upon how tired or distracted the parent is feeling in the moment.

Years after the fact, Denise realized that indulging her daughter's habit of interrupting conversations by whining was a big mistake. It had seemed so inconsequential when it began. It was easier for Denise to ignore her daughter or give in rather than take the time to stop her own conversation, point out to her daughter that she was interrupting, ask her daughter to wait, continue her conversation, and address her daughter after she was finished. Because she didn't take the time at the onset of her daughter's behavior, what she had now was a demanding, whiny, and, frankly, very annoying nine-year-old who had never learned to wait her turn. It was no wonder that Denise had frequent headaches while caring for her children and often found herself not enjoying their company.

Jane, a single mother and new client, came to me because she was experiencing problems at home with her three daughters. Her oldest daughter is a precocious and somewhat bossy fifteen-year-old whose significant academic, social, and athletic accomplishments were beginning to go to her head.

"Kathy's driving her sisters crazy with her bossiness, and she's starting to get a little mouthy with me, too. When I bring it up she looks at me as if I'm an idiot she has to tolerate."

"What does she do, specifically, that is annoying?" I asked.

"It's not any one thing. It's just little stuff, really. Like she'll shove Jessica out of her way if she's in a rush to get to her soccer game. If Jessica dares to say something, Kathy just acts like it's okay for her to do that because she's so important to her team and has to get out of the house. It's such a stupid little thing, but it leaves a bad taste in everyone's mouth."

"Nothing is too little if it leaves someone feeling badly," I said. "I know it seems insignificant in that moment, but it's actually a perfect situation to address Kathy's unacceptable behavior. You can say something immediately and be very specific. Tell Kathy that she's starting to act too big for her britches and that's it not an attractive quality. Tell her that being late for her soccer match is no excuse for being rude and that she owes Jessica an apology before she leaves. She'll probably look at you like you're making a big deal out of nothing, but that's okay. Stick to your guns, and tell her that manners are important in all situations, no matter what else is going on. Kathy needs to realize that people aren't going to buy into her idea that status is more important than being a good citizen."

■ *As generous as a parent tries to be with her patience, the reactive or manipulative adolescent will not be inspired to change her behavior. She will continue doing what she is doing.*

Generosity begets generosity in many walks of life, but not with an angry, resentful, uncommunicative adolescent who is seeking advantage over a parent the teen feels is too restrictive. Parents kid themselves when they believe that being "nicer" is the *solution* to their problems. Being nice is wonderful, and I've always believed that kindness is a critical ingredient to good relationships, but it has to be an integral, ongoing, and natural part of the relationship—not a vehicle used to gain specific responses from another party. When parents decide to bypass an issue, the teen won't see it as a patient, sympathetic gesture, but as an abdication of authority.

Sometimes a parent will find that the need to react more decisively or more firmly toward their acting-out adolescent is at odds with their personal belief system or set of family values. "I grew up in a family where we were taught to turn the other cheek and do everything we could to deal with problems peacefully," said one mother while discussing her difficulties raising a hotheaded, feisty teenage boy with lots of behavior and school-related problems. "I always believed in the philosophy of catching more bees with honey than with vinegar, but no matter how much I may think that way, my son sure doesn't, and that's where I feel like I'm at a loss. My way of dealing with him clearly isn't working—he's like a loose cannon these days—but I don't know what else to do. . . ."

This lovely woman, widowed, beleaguered, raising her only child alone, was stumped. She knew only one way to deal with conflict, and her son wasn't responding well. The situation is akin to the story of the carpenter whose only tool is a hammer, and everything that needs fixing begins to look like a nail. Limited by an interpersonal style that had little accommodation to contentiousness or resistance, Rebecca had hit a wall in the raising of her volatile son.

I told Rebecca, "Your son's personality and interpersonal style is very different from yours, and he's going to press you to stretch in ways you'll probably find very challenging, especially because you're raising him yourself. If your husband were still living, he might have been able to balance out your harmonious nature with a contrasting, more confrontational approach, but now you are going to have to cover both ends of the spectrum—soft and firm. I think that talking to Dan about how your upbringing *and* the loss of his dad have influenced your parenting would be a wonderful way for the two of you to begin rebuilding your relationship. Tell him how hard it will be for you to play the heavy, but let him know that in his beloved father's absence you will step up and do what needs doing. Your candor about something so meaningful to the two of you will have more impact on him than you could imagine."

■ *Repeatedly accommodating an adolescent's sullen mood or negative attitude allows her to avoid feeling accountable for how she affects other people.*

Everyone becomes unhappy or irritable or impatient at times. But most people try to keep their emotional state from putting a damper on everyone else's life, at least in any significant way—most people except the overly accommodated, moody adolescent. She feels entitled to impose her bad mood or bad attitude on anyone who dares to be around her. She wears her sneer, scowl, or frown on her sleeve, and makes sure that if you don't at least feel as miserable as she does, you will know exactly how miserable she is.

Parents who allow their teenager to dictate the mood around the house or dinner table are doing their child—and the family—a disservice. They may believe they are reducing the pressure on their already distressed child and giving him some "space" to come out of his funk. Unfortunately, they are neglecting to teach him that we all have a responsibility to be sensitive to our effect on the people around us, and while it is good to be genuine about our emotions and selectively open about our woes, it's not good to make everyone else suffer in kind. Learning how to communicate one's troubled inner life in a way that draws compassion from others and not exasperation is an exquisite skill. Parents should try to model and teach this behavior to their teenage children every opportunity they get.

▣ *Parents who try to get their teenager to feel sorry for them because of what the teen is "putting them through" compromise their parental authority and their dignity. The tactic won't work to change their teen's behavior, and the parents feel even more taken advantage of.*

Evoking genuine compassion, sensitivity, and accountability in an adolescent for the impact of her choices on others *is* a legitimate goal. Parents who act and speak with self-respect, rather than as someone to feel sorry for, will find respect mirrored by those around them.

Appealing blatantly to a teen's sympathies, however, undermines their respect for the parent. Any sympathies that are evoked are more likely to be pity rather than empathy, which doesn't help encourage changes in behavior or attitude.

Gary tried for longer than he should have to get Jared, his sixteen-year-old son, to stop snapping at his mother by appealing to his sympathies.

"Can't you see what you put your mother through when you talk to her like that?"

Jared would just look the other way and change the television channel.

"I'm talking to you," Gary would continue. "Why do you feel it's okay for you to say things that hurt her feelings?"

"I don't," replied Jared.

"Then why do you do it?"

"I don't know."

21

That was as far as Gary could ever get the conversation to go. The reason was because Gary was inadvertently supporting Jared's dismissal of his mother by talking to Jared about her as if she couldn't say these things to him herself. It was critical that Jared's mom herself address Jared's way of speaking to her, but in a different way than Gary did. If she says something that conveys *Go easy on me because you hurt my feelings when you talk to me like that,* she will not succeed in eliciting regard from Jared. A comment that communicates *Find a different way to air your grievances, because as an adult and as your mother, I won't tolerate being spoken to that way* is much more effective than Gary's remark that pulls for pity. A comment such as "Look, Jared, no one is having a good time here these days. We're fighting a lot. Can you pull the punches for a while and work with Dad and me on trying to get along a little better?" invites collaboration, self-restraint, and mutual respect.

PARENTS often say to me that they feel blindsided by the eruption of serious problems during their child's adolescence. They don't know where the defiance came from, or the impudence, or the evasiveness, or the deceitfulness. They are taken aback by their teenager's ability to be so confrontational, brazen, and smug.

"We never had these problems when Jimmy was in middle school," a parent will say to me. "I don't know what happened. . . ."

The problems were probably already there, but they were disguised by the child's youth or seeming innocence, which offered a hefty margin of error in his parents' eyes. In addition, the limited range of choices that a younger child has when compared to an adolescent protects that child from expressing the problem in more flagrant ways. It's easier to be defiant when you don't need your mom to tuck you in at night.

The good news here is that many of these problems are correctable. The *sad* news is that so many of them are avoidable in the first place. Despite what the long-standing traditions of American adolescent mythology say, teenagers are really good kids. They don't *have* to be argumentative, irascible, or disagreeable. They may not be easy, but they can be easier.

## 2

# How Teenagers Are Overindulged

There are influences other than family and parents that create conditions in which a child grows up too permissively. These influences are culture-bound and encourage qualities in the teenager that are (mistakenly) thought to be intrinsic to adolescence.

Our culture's long-standing romanticizing of the teenage years does this very well—we *wink wink* in the face of Luke's misadventures or display a tolerant smile in the face of Meredith's snippy greeting. "Oh, I got into tons of trouble when I was a kid," a father will say of his acting-out boy as reason not to intervene, "and I turned out all right." "What the heck," says the mother of a seventeen-year-old girl caught drinking with friends on the city's golf course. "It's one of her last chances to have fun before she becomes a grown-up and has to get serious about life. Besides, at least it wasn't pot."

No, it wasn't pot, but it was still illegal. It was also dangerous. How much booze? Who drove home? How much was *that* kid drinking? Where else and when do they go out drinking? The incident itself is, unfortunately, pretty common these days, but the response of the mother is poor. Her response says *No big deal, hon.* It says *Wake me up when you get into real trouble.* It says *Adulthood is a miserable time.* All terrible messages.

## Sociocultural Myths About Adolescence That Further Neutralize Parents' Authority and Confidence

Societies and cultures develop ideas about their people and communities that subsequently define how they are perceived. These conceptions are handed down from one generation to the next, becoming truths in the process. Many become an integral part of a society's thinking, shaping its members' reactions to common events. This has been the case with adolescence in America. Collective beliefs about this particular life stage and what those going through it do, think, and say have a lot to do with molding parents' and educators' beliefs about what is normal or expected behavior from adolescents. And, like any other collection of beliefs, some are valid, and some are not.

### ▣ *Myth #1: Teenagers Can't Help Being Moody and Should Be Excused for It*

Says who? Says an arrogant teenager who wants everyone to believe that her moodiness is something she is entitled to and cannot control. Says the unhappy teenager whose moodiness is driven not by her stage of life but by her chronic dis-

25

content. Says the alienated teenager who eschews contact from her concerned parents by responding with sour looks every time they make overtures of support. Or says the mother who can't bear to confront her teenager's moods again because it always results in another argument. Moreover, she inevitably feels guilty because she wonders if it's really *not* the child's fault (as the child so vehemently proclaims) and instead just a function of all those hormones running amok through her daughter's body.

The roller-coaster hormones *are* real, as are the roller-coaster relationships with boyfriends, girlfriends, and other friends; family; educators; and so on. There are also the haunting, and at times oppressive, self-doubts of adolescence, not to mention self-consciousness, self-absorption, and self-importance. Add to that ever-morphing bodies, separation fears, pimples, and proms, and *anyone* can manage to drum up a fair amount of sympathy for what teenagers go through. However, intermittent bouts of moodiness that blow over, are easily consoled, or otherwise don't oppress the household are one thing, but a wave of "bad mood" that sweeps up everybody in its wake is another. Before the parent realizes it, being a moody teenager has become an excuse to be a rude teenager.

Richard and Yolanda had just about given up trying to change their daughter's chronic moodiness around the house. Caitlin glowers, scowls, and nitpicks her way through most days. If they ask her what's wrong, she ignores them. If they press for a response, she snaps at them as they'd seen her do with her friends—those that remained.

"I guess I always figured that teenagers were supposed to be a little moody and inconsiderate," Richard said to me during a consultation. "I mean, that's what I've always heard, anyway. So I let a lot of it go and figure she'll grow out of it sooner or later. I didn't think it would do any good to force her to be less moody. We'd just end up fighting all the time."

"You probably would end up fighting all the time," I said to Richard and Yolanda, "*if* you were going to try and force her to feel something she doesn't." The answer *wasn't in trying to get Caitlin to feel differently,* but in *teaching her to respond differently to how she feels* when she is especially reactive or volatile. Caitlin hadn't a fraction of the interest her parents had in learning to respond more acceptably and would have been quite happy to continue ruling the roost with her moods. I told Richard and Yolanda it was up to them to find some way to make responding appropriately the more appealing choice for their daughter. They would need to establish consequences for her behavior—not for feeling moody, which is largely out of Caitlin's control—*but for her acts of rudeness,* which are completely under her control.

"You mean punish her every time she goes storming around the house, slamming cabinets?"

Not really, I said, adding that if they did, they'd only find themselves in another no-win power struggle over how loud is too loud for a cabinet to be slammed. Rather, the point would be to communicate to Caitlin that they and her siblings don't want to have to be subjected to her misery without at least being given the opportunity to try and help her be less miserable. If she was going to decide to reject their help and stay miserable for a while, which sometimes people prefer, she at least had to be miserable in a fashion that didn't perpetrate her mood on the household. She could, for instance, glower

### When Moodiness Is a Sign of a More Serious Problem

If a teenager appears excessively moody, it might be a sign that something's wrong. Parents should take time to consider that their son or daughter might be unhappy or very anxious about something, suffering from depression, or having major problems about which the parents are unaware. A worrisome degree of moodiness would include patches of dark or irritable moods that come almost daily, moodiness that stays for days on end several times a month, a period of moodiness that goes on for weeks and weeks, or anything else that just feels wrong. Parents should take the initiative to ask their teenagers about their moodiness, and even if the teen doesn't have a good answer, let her know that they are willing to help her through the difficult time but not willing to be the punching bag.

If the teen exclaims, *"Fine, I'll just keep everything to myself then!"* the parent can respond by saying, *"I'm not asking you to hide how you feel, and I think you know that. I'm asking you to be more responsible for how you let your moods affect everyone else. It's one thing to be unhappy, but another to snap at everyone in sight. You don't have to go through this by yourself. Let me help you."* Helping a son or daughter understand the difference between being open about how he or she feels and *acting out* on the bad feelings by being short with others is a gift that parent would be giving during this difficult phase.

No one should *assume* that a teenager's moodiness is necessarily a normal part of adolescence. Many teenagers will experience intense mood swings, and parents should be sensitive to this in a way that empathizes with how taxing and confusing it is for the teenager to feel so changeable all the time. However, parents still need to hold their son or daughter responsible for how they handle their mood swings. Being a teenager and having mood swings is not an excuse for the teenager to take out her irritability on her family members or friends.

all she wanted to in her room or out in the yard, but she could not glower at everyone through dinner. If she did, she'd be asked to eat in another room. She could slam all the soccer balls she wanted to along the concrete driveway wall, but if she banged around the kitchen enough to wake up everyone in the middle of the night after being asked not to, she'd be responsible to cover, for example, the morning household chores so that everyone who'd been woken up could sleep in a bit in the morning. She could ignore her friends' calls all she wanted (not because it's okay, but because there is no way for parents to control that, and, besides, the natural consequences of her friends' reactions will help affect her more convincingly than anything her parents could say), but she couldn't ignore the people in her household. If she did, she'd be told *right then and there* that she was being rude and that it wasn't appreciated, rather than everyone tolerating and excusing her behavior as part of "being a teenager."

### ▣ *Myth #2: Teenagers Don't Like Talking with Their Parents About Serious Issues or Concerns*

This myth has less to do with teenagers than it does any one person's discomfort discussing important or delicate matters. Adults who are comfortable talking about such matters in general probably have little difficulty talking about them with their teenage children.

Some parents who aren't comfortable talking with their kids communicate their discomfort in the process. The kid figures that because the parent is anxious, there must be something to be anxious about. Families unaccustomed to talking openly together about their thoughts, opinions, and reactions to the events or upcoming decisions in their lives wind up creating a bigger deal about important discussions. Some conversations with teenagers are always going to be more unsettling or embarrassing than others, and a fair share of them are averted, but the adolescent isn't the sole culprit here: Many parents avoid an imperative discussion in the hope that the issue will take care of itself.

Sometimes, a discussion gets off on the wrong foot and goes downhill from there. A teenager acts defensively or evasively. A parent patronizes or becomes judgmental. The adolescent reacts poorly in turn, and the parent gets angrier. The conversation becomes a lecture, parents start demanding answers, and patience with the teenager's (il)logic or perspective grows thin. The little bit of goodwill with which both parties might have started off evaporates, and parent and teenager are disappointed once again.

Fourteen-year-old Ryan is sullen and withdrawn and refuses to tell his parents anything about what's going on in his life. His parents don't like feeling so much in the dark but said to me, "We're not really a 'talk-y' kind of family. I mean, what can you say to a fourteen-year-old anyway?"

I told them that there is a lot you can say, including, *"You know, Ryan, we've never really been a talk-y kind of family, and I don't think your dad and I are particularly good at that sort of thing. But we probably ought to give it a try. You're fourteen now, and doing more stuff on your own. I don't want to be wondering what's going on with you all the time. I don't want to have to guess. Even now, when you look so sad or preoccupied or something, I don't know what about."*

Countless discussions bite the dust because a parent worries too much about saying the right thing. Believing that there is one "correct" way to discuss homework, sex, drinking, going out, coming home, and other topics of that ilk, they worry so much about saying the wrong thing that they say nothing at all. *Oh, never mind,* the mom thinks to herself. *I'll make a mess of things if I try to bring this up. I'll just wait for some other time when I have a better idea how to say what I want to say.* But by waiting for when she and her child can have the "right" discussion, they have none.

### ▣ *Sensitive topics*

One hurdle to many parent/teen discussions is not that teenagers and parents are less adept at talking about "deep" issues, but that the topics are either especially sensitive topics (i.e., sex) or especially secretive (sex, again, or drug and alcohol use). If a parent is having a tough time figuring out where to start one of these conversations, I'd encourage her to start anywhere, letting her child know that she's having difficulty finding the right words but that she feels it's more important to have some kind of conversation—even an awkward one—than to have the "right" one. It will also take pressure off the teenager to have the right or the perfect response. If a parent doesn't know what question to ask or how to ask it, she should tell her child what it is she wants to understand better about him or his activities or his social life. She can ask her son what questions *he* thinks she should be asking to find those things out. Making the discussion collaborative in its inquiry sets up a collaborative tone for the teenager's response and any subsequent discussion.

If the discussion starts to get heated, parents can pause and say something like, *"Look, we're starting down a road that I don't want to go down. Let's stop and regroup. I really want to talk more about this, but I don't want this issue to come between us. Will you start this conversation over with me?"* This is a nice way to stop the degeneration of the discussion without laying blame and leaves an easy way to restart.

A parent who feels that he and his teenager have had a good interaction around a challenging topic should let the teen know that he thinks so. Kids appreciate hearing that their parents have enjoyed an experience of learning more about them, and it will encourage more of the same. Parents should avoid, however, shining too bright a light on it or becoming very congratulatory, as many adolescents can become uncomfortable when the parent-child connection is the center of attention. It's too emotionally intimate for most.

◼ *Myth #3: Teenagers Need a Lot of Free Rein to Learn How to Make Decisions on Their Own*

Raising a teenager who can make decisions on her own is easy. Raising one who makes *good* decisions on her own takes a little more doing.

Kids learn to make good decisions by observing the people close to them making a decision and bearing its positive or negative consequences. Good judgment and accountability are qualities handed down from one generation to the next by setting examples. Kids need parents' and other elders' help in shaping their discretion, prudence, patience, and reflection.

A mom of a seventeen-year-old girl who wished to drop

out of school and get an apartment with three girlfriends said:

> "I want my child to grow up able to make her own decisions. If I'm always putting my two cents in, how will she ever learn? Besides, her values should be her own and not mine or her dad's. I want to raise an independent person, not a clone who does things because that's what her parents do. She'll learn better by making her own mistakes than by my telling her what I think all the time."

But values don't form without influence, and if it's not the parents' influence, it will be someone else's—savory characters or not. Why would a parent hold her and her husband's values in such little regard? Don't they *want* their daughter to adopt the more important of their values, at least for starters, before she fashions them to her own personality and needs as she becomes more independent? If not theirs, then whose?

This parent's thinking is reminiscent of what author Kay Hymowitz, in her book *Ready or Not: What Happens When We Treat Children As Small Adults* (Encounter Books, San Francisco, 2000), refers to as an ideology of *anticulturalism*. An outgrowth of the civil rights movement and other liberation movements of the 1960s (women, gays), anticulturalism depicts kids, too, as an oppressed minority in need of liberation. Parental protectiveness is viewed as "an ideology of control," and parents' attempts to mold the character of the young is seen as a "wrongful use of power by the strong against the weak." (U.S. News & World Report, Nov. 1, 1999, p. 26)

As improbable as such a philosophy might appear, Hymowitz contends that it has, in fact, spread widely in this country over the past forty years, filtering down to family life and education. Parents and educators are encouraged to stimulate children's appetites for learning, but admonished not to give too much shape and meaning to the process. The result is the reduction of these critical figures in children's lives to being "cultural and moral bystanders." (U.S. News & World Report, Nov. 1, 1999, p. 26)

Louise Kaplan, in her book *Adolescence: The Farewell to Childhood* (Jason Aronson, Inc., 1986), similarly speaks of the ways in which certain social idealists, viewing adolescence as more of a social construction, an artificial prolongation of childhood rather than a differentiated life stage, see a paradox in the legal arrangements we have in place to protect our minors. They call attention to the discrepancies between the professed aims to protect children and what they believe is an insidious suppression. Compulsory education, child-labor laws, and the concept of juvenile delinquency are seen by these idealists as having produced not children protected from the exigencies of adult responsibility, but "an underworld of disenfranchised children and youths, who now view themselves as prisoners of a social system that promises success, power, [and] income in exchange for delaying adult sexual and legal status but in fact delivers very little of these advantages to most children." (p. 44)

I don't agree with that position. I find the protections we have in place for our minors both purposeful and balanced. Few kids would actually want to fend for themselves, and none should ever have to. But Hymowitz's and Kaplan's descriptions of these more extreme points of view shed an informed light on the parenting styles and choices made by mothers and fathers who believe that less parenting is, somehow, more. The results though, I fear, are not precociously enlightened children but something like the boy in *The Philadelphia Inquirer* (6/20/01) who insists that he had the right to participate in his high school graduation ceremonies in spite of his profane tirade when told he needed to change out of his work boots. His father's response? Not *"Gee, I'm sorry and embarrassed for him that he reacted so poorly"* or *"Well, it's really too bad, and maybe he'll have learned that there are better ways to get your point across,"* but rather "[The school] needed one more hour and then he'd be out of high school. They just had to wait until they reached the W's and then he'd be out." (p. B3) Furthermore, the boy and his father are considering a lawsuit against the school.

### LEARNING LIFE VALUES

- A parent shouldn't stop trying to impart important life values to his or her teenager just because the teenager acts as if he doesn't need them. Children and adolescents need parents, educators, and other influential adults in their lives to regularly lend meaning to their experiences so that they can make sense of them and process them in healthy ways. When kids are allowed to do that on their own too often, they get disorganized and lost. They start thinking that they know more than they really do, can decide more than they should, and can handle more than they are able. They make bad decisions and bear the consequences without benefit of parental support and redirection. They will not always learn from their mistakes as well as they will from their parents because some lessons are better taught at home.

▪ Parents need to remember that lending a perspective is different from imposing one. They need to modify the way they talk about values and choices with their sons and daughters as they transition from childhood to adolescence. While a parent may have lectured to a child about respect for others, the value of education, or the dangers of drug use, covering these issues with a teen needs to be in the form of a dialogue; the message is the same, but the format is different. The parents haven't changed their allegiance to their message about respect, schooling, or drugs, nor their expectation that their child will make sound choices and respect the parents' preferences while living in their home. However, there is also a quiet understanding that the teenager will probably be putting those values to various tests as he or she defines his or her own moral and ethical base throughout the late teenage and early adulthood years.

▪ It is useful for parents to create distinctions between those decisions their adolescent makes which they can tolerate even if they disagree with it (i.e., kid's choice of one summer job over another) and those which they feel they cannot (i.e., kid's wish to drop out of school). This helps parents recognize their decreasing control and allows the adolescent safe, manageable opportunities to experiment with making bigger decisions while he still has some backup from home.

▪ Parents should resist the temptation to bow out of their responsibilities of continuing to be involved in their teenager's life by buying into the belief that teens need to learn to make decisions on their own. Providing opportunities for kids to expand their range of independent functioning while offering support the teenager appreciates and doesn't eschew is one of a parent's greatest balancing acts. One great radio/television public service announcement these days says it well: *"Ask what, who, where, how. It's not pestering. It's parenting."*

## 3

# WHY PARENTS BACK DOWN

Society and culture aren't the strongest influences affecting how children are raised in America. That role is reserved for the people most closely involved in a child's upbringing. This includes mothers and fathers, but also aunts and uncles, grandparents and godparents, who all bring to the parenting mix their own set of psychological and emotional conditions that operate on the young person's burgeoning character and soul.

These people, in turn, have been shaped by the life circumstances and personalities of their own caregivers. By recognizing these past influences and personality styles, parents can modify or override their personal tendencies in order to effectively, confidently, flexibly, and resourcefully parent a teen.

## Conflict-Avoidant Personality Style

Conflict makes some people so uncomfortable that they will do most anything to avoid it. In the case of parents with unruly teenagers, that can include ignoring, downgrading, or glossing over problems that cry out for attention, acquiescing to the teenager for the sake of ending the argument or badgering, or subjugating their own judgment to the story spun by the teenager who has much to gain by getting her parents to look the other way.

A conflict-avoidant parent is an easy match for a teenager who tries to bully her way in the family with her moods, belligerence, or verbal intimidation. If the parent is unable to stand her ground and stick to the limits that have been set, the teen will take further and further advantage. A vicious cycle ensues as the parent who tried to avoid the conflict when the conflict was smaller backs off further from the problem as it grows larger under the teenager's expanding reign of power.

■ *"I'm always worried about saying the 'wrong' thing and then having to deal with my daughter's reaction."*

The parents of fifteen-year-old Lydia were desperate to reach their daughter and stem the flood of her angry outbursts and destructive tantrums. But each time they'd try to talk with her, Lydia would get angrier and more destructive. Worried that being firmer with her, or more frank about their concerns, would agitate their daughter even more, Lydia's parents opted for quiet reproaches, hoping that would engender more cooperation.

"I know I come off as a softie sometimes," Lydia's mom said, "but I keep thinking that by being more patient, she'll eventually become a little more reasonable."

She didn't—until Lydia's mom became more insistent that

Lydia not make family members the targets of her hysterical rages.

---

■ *"During an argument, I'm afraid I'm going to end up angrier than my teenager."*

Some adolescents have learned to push their parents' buttons so well that when the parent does press an issue, he or she becomes angrier and more out of control than the child.

"I can't stand to argue with him anymore," one despairing parent confided in me after her son walked out of my office. "He knows that I feel guilty about being a single mom and always manages to turn a situation around so that I end up feeling even more guilty—like his problems are all my fault or something!"

Warren, father of sixteen-year-old Mark, is at his wit's end over his son. "He's a master at getting my ire up. Whenever we get into an argument, Mark manages to get me going so badly that I end up stomping around, trying ridiculously to make my point while he sits there calmly, observing. I think he enjoys seeing me get more bent out of shape than he is."

Warren is probably right. Mark probably loves seeing his dad stomp around the house, but not because he simply wants his dad to be angry. He is gratified because, psychologically, it accomplishes several things:

- it turns the focus from him onto his father,

- it makes his father look more "out of control" than he is (any adolescent's definition of a coup d'etat),

- it successfully engenders within the father the feelings and agitation that Mark feels inside—he is not so alone in his experience, and

- it evokes emotion (any will do) from a parent who has tried so hard to be rational that he has lost touch with his more genuine and candid side.

---

▣ *"I worry that things will get out of hand and my son will just lose it."*

Some parents worry that their teenager could become so out of control that she could hurt herself, hurt someone else, or become physically destructive. That's what stopped Nina's parents in their tracks every time.

"The last time we told Nina that she couldn't go to a concert she'd been planning to attend, she spent the whole night in her room cutting up her arms with a pocket knife. We didn't even find out about it until the morning. We just can't take that chance again, but we have to set some limits, don't we?" her mom wondered.

Nina's mother was correct. No parent can effectively decide how to respond to a problem based on what his or her child might or might not do. Parents must make decisions based on what is in the best interests of that child. Once they make their decision, they then have to control all possibilities. They could say:

"Nina, the last time we said no to you, you spent the night in your room cutting up your arms. We can't be intimidated

41

into saying yes to things we don't think you should be doing, but we also can't take a chance that you'll spend the night again in your room with a pocket knife. So you'll be camping out with us on our bedroom floor tonight and the next night and so on until we don't feel the need to worry."

Never negotiate with a terrorist.

▣ *"Sometimes, I worry so much about the effect the arguing is having on our other kids that I just back off."*

Parents often drop an issue in order to prevent other family members from being drawn into the problems they are having with the one child or from having to deal with the miserable fallout from protracted conflict. Kim's parents did this for years, before they learned that the gains were short-lived and served only to increase Kim's control over the family's activities.

"Kim's tantrums were not only disrupting our lives but the lives of her three sisters as well," said Kim's mother, describing her daughter's tendency to physically strike out at her parents when confronted and never think twice about causing a scene in restaurants, in parking lots, or at family functions. "Sometimes we just drop the whole issue because we can't bear to have her keep carrying on."

"If Kim's going to pull shenanigans like that, she loses the opportunity to go out," I told Kim's parents.

"But sometimes I'm not even sure she wants to be out with us," her dad replied.

"Maybe she doesn't. But then it's up to her to tell you that she doesn't like going out with her family and why that is. You can help by asking her if what you think might be true *is* true. Maybe she feels left out because of her prior antics. Maybe she feels self-conscious if she *doesn't* pull any antics because everyone will think she's being such a 'good girl.' Maybe she gets bored or restless or feels that because she's messed up so many times she can't possibly expect anyone to take her suggestions for where to go or what to do seriously. Maybe she thinks no one wants her to come along anymore. Talk to her, and give her a face-saving way out of the mess she's created for herself."

Zachary was a wizard at detecting just how to exquisitely spoil Thanksgiving dinner at Grandma's house. He began each year by disappearing approximately one-half hour before departure time and reappearing one hour after the family was supposed to have left. At dinner he was snide, aloof, and taunting.

"Have you hired a baby-sitter for this year's dinner?" I asked Zachary's parents.

"Baby-sitter? Janet, he's fifteen," replied Zachary's mom.

"Yup. But he's not acting like he's fifteen. And more important, he's playing you, and he's playing Grandma. It's calculated, and it's mean. Find a sitter, and put her on retainer for the day and evening. Tell Zachary that this year you will all be leaving on time, and there will be no waiting around for him. When Zachary disappears at departure time, you do, too—to Grandma's house. Don't let him hold you hostage to his game-playing. Let him come home to a baby-sitter and a microwaved turkey pot pie instead of a family waiting on his every move. I bet next year he'll be a little more ready to leave on time."

## Passive Interaction Style

☐ *"I'm just too tired/hopeless/overwhelmed . . . ."*

Seventeen-year-old Ray had been running his dad ragged for the past six months and was about to lose this last and most vital support left in his dwindling circle of friends and fans. Charming and gregarious, this boy had shown no mercy to his family in his quest for bigger thrills and more fanciful escapes from capture. Ray repeatedly ignored curfew, waved off groundings, and informed no one of his after-school whereabouts. Now he'd been caught smashing neighbors' mailboxes, smoking marijuana, and joyriding. His dad had tried everything he knew to do to help his son. He sat in my office, threw up his hands, and said, "I'm sick and tired of worrying more about his well-being than he is. I have his younger brother to worry about, you know, and he's too good to be getting the short end of the stick here."

Sadly, Ray had pushed the envelope too far and was losing his best chance to pull things together. Ray's dad was raising the two boys alone and had few resources to draw on once his own were exhausted. He needed some support from me, some ideas for bringing other family members onboard to assist in more closely supervising Ray, and, importantly, permission to let Ray's problems be Ray's problems for a little while, in spite of the potential consequences. There are times when systems outside the family, such as the juvenile justice or legal systems, are needed to make the kind of stronger impression on a too-casual teenager that he (hopefully) will find harder to dismiss.

That's, finally, what made the difference for Ray that his dad and I couldn't make. Busted for marijuana possession and driving without a license, the overnight lock-up Ray endured sent him home with his tail between his legs. When his dad gave him the choice to go into drug rehabilitation or be sent out for residential placement, Ray chose the former. He and his dad still wrestle over rules, behavior, and matters of control, but Ray's understanding that his father won't hesitate to use more restrictive services helped tone down some of Ray's more outrageous behaviors.

▣ *"I'm worried that I'll take things too far. . . ."*

It's understandable that a parent whose own temper or aggressiveness can go too far will have trouble defining appropriate lines of assertiveness. One result is that the parent, as a way of protecting everyone, will not act assertively enough when his or her children need him to. He or she backs off areas of potential conflict to the point of disappearing altogether, defers the responsibilities of child guidance and discipline excessively and perhaps exclusively to a spouse, and overlooks many situations with their teenager that call out for attention and intervention. Parenting less independently and more as a *team* with a spouse or, if a single parent, another close relative helps the volatile adult avoid throwing out the baby with the bathwater and to continue serving in his or her parenting role. Community-based mental heath agencies and family medical practices, as well as some high school guidance offices, can serve as resources for parents seeking information on parenting groups or support services. Local newspapers also usually have listings for workshops and other types of educational programs.

## Family of Origin Issues

▣ *"What happened to me when I was growing up will never happen to my children."*

An adult whose parents were very harsh in their parenting and disciplining may vow never to show or tolerate such harshness in her own family. The reaction may be so extreme, however, that they go overboard, and in the spirit of protecting their children from experiencing what they experienced, they create a family atmosphere that is *too* charitable and lenient. The kids, not appreciating that their parent has adopted a particular parenting style for their express benefit, see only liberties and respond the only way that one can expect them to—by testing these liberties. If an adolescent's parents confuse the idea of being firm about rules and limits with being mean or overbearing, the situation is ripe for the teen to pitch the balance of power in his favor. The parents wonder why they feel so trampled when all they've done is try to be nice.

▣ *"That's how my parents handled things, and it was good enough for me."*

Lost in the belief that they only know what they have experienced themselves, these parents underestimate the breadth of child-rearing information they have been exposed to over the years (friends, relatives, books, magazines, news reports, television, *personal experience*) that can help them modify their fundamental and early beliefs about family life and the raising of kids. For parents whose own parents were lax about rules or indulgent, the cycle then perpetuates.

It's important to realize, though, that times are different, our communities are different, and kids are different. What worked in the past may not work now. It's no slap in any parent's face to try and improve upon the earlier model, no matter how excellent it may have been.

## Marital Tensions

▣ *"If truth be told, I want my kids to love me more than they love their father."*

No one will admit to doing this, but it happens, because the effects are seen all the time. Kids work the gap between parents who vie for their favor, preference, or emotional loyalty. Knowing that each parent will want to be seen as the better, kinder, smarter, healthier, or more understanding of the two, such kids have field days playing off one parent's efforts to undermine the authority, dignity, or power of the other.

▣ *"I am willing to undermine my child in order to get back at my spouse."*

Revenge is often too sweet for some parents to resist, and he or she compromises the needs of the child or teenager in the hopes of aggravating, belittling, or otherwise getting back at a husband or wife.

In both this example and the preceding one, the parent is unable to do the right thing for the child because the need to win some sort of psychological victory over the spouse is too strong. Many parents who play these destructive games aren't consciously aware of it. Those who are find ways to justify their actions, or do them anyway despite their knowledge that it hurts the kids. For the individual who is capable of acting this way, it takes great discipline and self-awareness to deny oneself the opportunity to get back at a spouse with whom he or she is *that* angry. No relationship ever really improves by showing up the other person, though, and the kids suffer miserably from the hostility and spite on display. Parents need to make every effort to protect their children from the uglier side of their relationships and deal with their differences in a more constructive and direct fashion.

There are other kinds of chronic marital tensions affecting family life that aren't as vengeful as the ones described earlier. Recurring disagreements, gradual estrangement, or the loss of any sense of "partnership" between husband and wife can dampen the quality of family life within the home as well as the parents' ability to work together on raising their adolescent son or daughter. Presenting a *coordinated* front, even if not in total agreement with one another, is an essential task of parents managing the more challenging teenager described in this book.

## Making Up for Something Else

Adults' parenting styles can easily be affected by their attempts to make up for something they feel is missing in their lives or in the lives of their children. Compensating for an unsatisfactory adolescence of their own, or for not being as available to their child as they think they should be, or for the too-stern demeanor of a grumpy spouse can all have the effect of rendering parents excessively lenient. The following are ways in which a mother or father can allow themselves to believe they are supporting or benefiting their teenagers when, in fact, they are further compromising the teen's abilities to be responsible for themselves.

▣ *"I don't always say no when I should because I feel guilty about working too hard/being too irritable around the house/always missing the school concerts/not being the parent I think I should be. . . ."*

Guilt has the power to make people do all types of things, some good and some bad. Sometimes the motive is good and kind but the outcome unproductive, and that's often the case when a parent tries to make up for what they haven't done by doing too much of something else. Parents who try to make up for their sixty-hour workweek or the bad mood they've been in because they are fighting with their spouse or boss or mother may find it easier to express their "apologies" by letting their teen's poor behavior slide than by directly expressing their feelings about not having been a better-tempered mom or more available dad. If their temper or unavailability is the problem the parent worries that it is, saying something directly won't be revealing anything the teenager hasn't thought of herself; the parent's self-disclosure and candor serves as a beautiful gesture of penance. If it turns out that the teenager hasn't felt the parent to have been remiss, it still is a wonderful lesson for the child about self-reflection and accountability in relationships.

▣ *"I often feel as if I have to make up for my husband, who's sometimes so tough with the kids."*

When one parent is a little too severe, occasionally the other parent will feel a need to make up for it by being a little too nice. Unfortunately, too nice translates too easily into being too forgiving. With the wrong teenager, the kind who takes advantage of a parent's softer side, this attempt to balance out the parenting styles backfires.

"I feel bad for my son because my husband is just so gruff and hard with him. I try to make up for it by being extra nice," says the mother of a sixteen-year-old boy who clashes regularly and heavily with his chronically ill-tempered father.

I tell this mom that her son needs parents who will be simultaneously firm and empathic with him, and neither will be attained by the parents' moving in opposition to each others' stance. It would be better, I explain, for her to help her son depersonalize his father's stern demeanor, or even possibly see through the chronic gruffness as one of his father's flaws but as perhaps the only way he knows how to show concern. Denying the gruffness in the boy's father's message will only alienate them further, so it's important that she validate his experience without trying to protect him from it. She also needs to stop protecting her husband from his own bad temper, gently confront him about it without shaming him, and help him recognize the impact it is having on their son and on their father-son relationship.

▣ *"I wasn't popular with teenagers the first go-round, so I thought I might try it again while I had the chance."*

If adults were given an opportunity to rewrite their adolescence, there would be many takers. Few had the one they'd hoped to have, and many had the one they'd dreaded. Those who had a negative experience probably felt, for extended periods of time, that they didn't fit in, that the other kids by and large didn't like them, or that they somehow, for some reason, didn't "get" it.

Most of us manage to get through this experience and eventually find a circle of kids with whom we do fit in. We grow into well-adjusted adults in spite of our exclusion from high school's "A" crowd. But some never forget that feeling of being on the outside looking in, and when they find an opportunity later in life to yuk it up with those who *are* in, they jump on it.

Some parents like to play the fun buddy to their teenager's friends, or come off as a "cool" dad or mom. They do it to gratify a long-standing unmet need to be accepted and fit in with teenagers, or sometimes, to gain points with their kids. In doing so, they are tempted to say yes when they should say no, tolerate inappropriate intrusions on their time or space, or laugh off the smug response when they should say *Excuse me, Sophie, what did I hear you say?*

# 4

# HOW PARENTS LOSE CREDIBILITY

"I don't have problems getting anyone else to listen to me," says Nancy, a thirty-six-year-old executive and mom whose thirteen-year-old daughter argues nearly every request she makes of her. "But if I ask Kelly to clean her room or start her homework, I get a look like you wouldn't believe and some reason why it's not a good time. When I insist, she rolls her eyes at me and mumbles things under her breath. I can never get out of her what these mumblings are, but I'm certain they're not pretty. And she's only thirteen! What am I going to have on my hands when she's sixteen, seventeen?"

Nancy is correct to want to begin changing things now in order to prevent more complex problems later. Kelly has already learned that rolling her eyes and mumbling under her breath are okay. She knows her mom doesn't approve of these behaviors, but they are okay in the sense that her mom is not going to address them directly. Her mom always presses the issue of cleaning her room and doing her homework, not Kelly's disrespectful manner. Kelly's mom, like so many parents, is not addressing the *quality* of her teenager's interactions, but focusing on the "content" of the disagreement. When Nancy makes a vague reference to Kelly about being disrespectful, Kelly doesn't connect it to the mumbling names under her breath or her snarly responses. She just thinks her mom is being picky.

"Oh, it's only a name mumbled under her breath," a parent might say if asked why she doesn't press her daughter about the way she speaks back to her. "How big of a deal is that? It's not like she's saying it to my face."

The kid *is* saying it to the parent's face. She keeps it unintelligible so she can't be called to account for the name. She knows that the parent knows she was called a name, and the teen feels she's gotten away with something.

Some parents worry about addressing so many aspects of their teenager's poor relating habits. Fearing constant conflict, they opt to "choose their battles" and let the less overtly offensive things slide.

Unfortunately, though, in the spirit of choosing battles, parents let too many go because there are too many issues to begin with. In this time of busy and beleaguered parents and kids, family members have lost the art of talking with one another, made habits out of becoming swiftly defensive, and wound up learning how to work their computers, Palm Pilots, and compact disc players better than they know how to develop close, genuine relationships. No one has time for what really matters. We feel sorry for our kids because they are depressed, violent, and lonely; we feel sorry for ourselves because we are overworked and unhappy. One way we compensate for that is to create family cultures of indulgence, where the kids are spoiled, not so much with material goods,

but with too many allowances for their inappropriate interactions with others or their lack of accountability for the impact of their demeanor, actions, and choices on those around
them.


"Oh, I really wasn't thinking anything about it, to be honest
with you," one mom said to me during a session when I inquired about her letting her fourteen-year-old son wander
over to my desk and handle some books I'd been reviewing.
"He's a little hyperactive, and has ADD, you know. He doesn't
mean anything by it. Jeremy, honey, leave Janet's stuff alone
and come sit down."

I'm sure Jeremy doesn't mean anything by it. He never
meant to offend. But he has never learned the difference between having a neurobehavioral condition that makes you
distractible and *want* to get up and do something, and the
courtesy of not handling someone else's private things without first asking—essentially, *of not doing something even though
you want to.* By fourteen, he should have been taught the difference.

Handling Jeremy's impulsiveness in the way his mom did is
one way a parent loses credibility for her judgment and authority in the eyes of her children. Kids know when they've
been given a bye. They may like it, but they don't respect it.
They are good at discerning the difference between a parent
who makes excuses for their distractibility, forgetfulness, or
lack of self-restraint and one who tries to help them to compensate for their deficit while still holding them accountable
for relating and acting appropriately.

## Losing Credibility

Overprotecting one's child or adolescent from the natural consequences of his own psychological shortcomings or vulnerabilities is one way of losing parental credibility. Trying too hard to be the "good" mom or the "fun" dad are other ways; both backfire. So may efforts to always say or do the "right" thing, or be the "big" help, or disguise feeling out of control when life throws its curves. Here are other ways, largely stemmimg from a parent's wish to stay on his or her kid's "good side":

■ *Soliciting their teenager's approval*

From a very young age, kids can pick out the adult who tries too hard to be liked. They can even pick out the one who doesn't think he or she is trying too hard. They know by the way the individual speaks to them, tries or doesn't try to get their attention, responds spontaneously (or not) to their antics, and maintains a sense of humor that isn't patronizing.

Parents who try to solicit a teenager's approval or affection by being especially nice or empathic or "cool" are destined not to be taken seriously. A self-respecting person carries herself with a demeanor that kids and adults both find compelling, but a person who feels she needs to convince another that she is worth liking loses the race at the start gate.

"Anytime I'd, like, be really good for a while, my mom would get really nice to me," Natalie confided in me. "Weird nice, though, not like the kind that's, you know, regular. It was like she was so happy that I was being 'good,' and so worried

I'd go back to messing up, that she would start acting in ways so that I'd never be angry with her. It's like she tried to be all nice and perfect, but it just made me feel like I didn't really respect her. I hate when she does that."

Natalie was perceptively describing her mother's change in countenance whenever Natalie would behave. Natalie's mom, Cheryl, *was* relieved by her daughter's change in behavior. She was so relieved that she wound up trying too hard to keep Natalie happy. She thought that if she were successful, Natalie would be less inclined to begin acting up again. Unfortunately, Natalie's mom was wrong; her "carefulness" around Natalie and reluctance to risk any conflict or problem engendered a disrespect that only served to put Natalie off and increase the chance of her acting up again.

Parents find themselves in this compromised position for a variety of reasons. Some believe erroneously that the currency of interpersonal power is approval, rather than respect, and spend time cultivating the former at the expense of the latter. Others simply confuse being liked with being respected and settle for the first, believing they have the second. Yet others have such a shaky self-concept as "parent in charge" that they don't trust their own natural authority to be sufficient to gain and carry their teenager's consideration. Once a parent tries to gain influence by trying to convince her adolescent to view her as especially and extraordinarily great or fun or nice, she has communicated that these qualities are not evident (or perhaps even present) in her being and actions. The typical adolescent responds first with pleasure, then with gradual boredom, and possibly, eventually, with contempt.

PARENTS CAN MAINTAIN CREDIBILITY:

- By bearing in mind that teenagers are savvy purveyors of human character and can easily recognize when someone is working to win their approval.

- By positioning themselves as the head of the household who cares less about what the teen thinks of them than whether or not that teenager is growing up to be the kind of person they would be proud to have raised.

- If a parent thinks that his teen will notice a striking difference in his manner if he were to become less obliging and solicitous, then he should say something about it to the teenager. He should say, with confident candor and even some humor, that he'd been thinking for some time that if he got more on his daughter's better side, he'd get more co-operation, but that now he realizes that it has been only making the problem worse. The father can go on to explain that he is going back to his old way of being a "regular" dad, and that he'll try some other way of smoothing things out at home. He should then smile, sit back, and wait for his daughter to respond.

### ▣ *Being too "careful"*

Adolescents know almost immediately when their parents begin worrying about saying or doing the "wrong" thing. Parents and adolescents perceive a "wrong" thing to be any remark or action that causes the adolescent to become upset or angry, which is often unfortunate but necessary. However, the only *really* wrong thing is saying something that's mean or

57

careless. Poor timing and poor wording can happen to any-body; we all do the best we can and apologize when we miss. The partner in the conversation also has his or her own re-sponsibilities—to accept the apology and not use the other person's stumble as an excuse to terminate a discussion.

Parenting that is *too* careful communicates to kids that the parent has lost confidence in himself or herself to effectively manage situations in which the kid gets upset or angry. This is a very enticing invitation to an adolescent who wants to shake things up at home. Playing on the parent's reluctance to speak or act, the kid has a field day.

### HOW TO BECOME LESS "CAREFUL":

- Worrying too much about the effect one's words and ac-tions will have on a volatile, defensive adolescent will cramp anyone's parenting. A parent's sensitivities about communicating are better directed toward filtering out words, phrases, and tones that could be expected to make *anyone* upset. In this way, a parent frees herself from being responsible for her adolescent's reaction and assumes a more appropriate (and manageable) scope of responsibility for communicating her concerns or disagreements in a way that another person can hear. How the child chooses to re-spond is up to him or her, but at least a parent can hold up her end by delivering the message in a palatable way. Par-ents don't need to worry about being careful if they refrain from teasing, getting sarcastic, being too abrupt, speaking over their teenager, jumping to conclusions, dismissing the teen's perspective out of hand, making fun, being aloof or rejecting, or saying things designed to shame. As far as the kid not liking *what* the parent has to say—well, you can't control that. Trying to soft-pedal the things that need saying or limits that need setting will yield only unsatisfactory results. Kids can better (even if silently and privately) appreciate parameters established by their parents in a spirit of humanity and respect, even if they feel the need to act as though they don't.

• If parents are dealing with an adolescent who could conceivably become violent or destructive, they need to have a structure in place that could accommodate that situation and keep it contained or at least safe. They should be prepared either to have the adolescent physically restrained, by the parents and/or other adults who are readily accessible (or even "on call"), or to call the police. Calling the police on your own child is a nightmare no parent likes to consider, but the willingness to do so, stated clearly to the teen, can mean the difference between parenting firmly and with impact and watching one's child destroy lives, including his own.

### ▣ *Trying to solve their teenager's problems for them*

Parents who are desperate to see their teenager's problems resolved can become vulnerable to trying to solve them for him. Despite the good intentions, the results are usually pretty disappointing for everyone involved. Mom and Dad are perpetually exasperated by their inability either to mobilize their teenager or get the problem(s) solved, and the teenager, in the wake of his parent's overinvolvement, becomes more passive as well as resentful of his parents' intrusions.

"But he kept saying that he wanted to graduate on time," said Beth about her seventeen-year-old son, Max, who, despite his proclamations, was managing to put his graduation at risk by repeatedly arriving late for his major subjects, forgetting to bring in his completed assignments, and not turning in final projects. "I started to get so worried that he might actually fail that my husband and I gave him the use of one of our cars, just so he'd be sure to get to school on time. He's walked for years. We live only a few blocks from the high school, but he's still late! I even started researching one of his projects for him just to get him motivated to start it, but he hasn't really done anything with that, either. It's ridiculous for him to fail. He's always been a good student, plus, he's got this great summer planned. I just can't believe this."

Beth was working too hard to get Max to graduate on time, and he was not working hard enough. That was only the half of it. It turned out that she and Max's dad, Larry, had established a routine for making sure Max was waking up on time and getting out of bed. The routine involved each of them getting up early on alternate mornings in order to check that Max had heard his alarm and hadn't fallen back to sleep. They had also begun supervising his homework, something they stopped doing for Max when he was in grade school.

Enough, I told Beth. She and Larry had to stop. Not only were their efforts not working, but Max was becoming more and more *in*active as a senior high school student. Clearly, Max was putting the brakes on getting out of school, and I told them that their efforts would be much better spent candidly discussing with Max why he was apparently sacrificing his graduation.

"But he denies not wanting to graduate," responded Beth. "He says he's just having trouble getting everything done."

"Then what I'd say to him is this, 'Look, Max, I know you keep saying that you want to finish on time, but your actions tell a different story. I want to believe you when you say you want to graduate, but I worry that there's something else going on and that something is causing you to risk failing two major subjects for the first time in your life. You are perfectly capable of getting yourself up in the morning and to school on time, so Dad and I are stopping the wake-up calls. You've also been doing your own homework—and doing it well, mind you—for the past decade. We think you can manage for these next couple of months. So barring any genuine help you need from us, you're on your own to finish or not finish.' "

"Janet, he can't *not* finish high school!"

"Why not?" I asked.

"Well, it's just ridiculous. He can pass."

"It *is* ridiculous, and of course he can pass. That's my point. You and Larry are doing things for Max that he can and needs to do for himself. As long as graduating on time remains more important to you than to Max, you'll find yourselves hostage to every bad choice of his that puts him more behind the eight ball."

"We're all supposed to go away, too. The whole month of July. We have a cabin in the mountains. We go every year. He won't be able to go if he has to make up his courses. What do we do about that?"

"Nothing. You guys go, and Max stays home and goes to summer school, or with a relative in town and takes public transportation to classes. Just make sure Max is aware of all this so he can make informed decisions."

"Oh boy," sighed Beth.

Something else was the matter. "What is it?"

"I think it might have something to do with having to go up to the cabin. I think he doesn't want to go this year."

"Doesn't Max have a better way of saying *No thank you Mom and Dad, I'd like to try doing something else this July if that's all right with you*"?

"Yup, he sure does. But unfortunately his dad has no way to say *Sure Max, that's fine for you to do something independently of the family. Tell us what you have in mind, and Mom and I will see what we think.*"

Now it was my turn to say "Oh boy." With the situation illuminated by Beth's insight into her husband's difficulties letting Max grow up and become more independent from the family, it was easier to both make "sense" of Max's seemingly irrational behavior, and direct my consultation to this family in useful ways.

■ *Putting a stop to unhelpful problem-solving*

Parents are better off thinking in terms of being an *accessory* to problem-solving efforts rather than the impetus. Efforts can be as strong, thorough, and enduring as the parent feels is necessary, but they need to stop short of initiating or completing acts that the adolescent should be doing for herself. Serving as the memory bank or courier for one's forgetful teenager will not help her remember or become more responsible. Repeatedly bailing a kid out of the legal, social, or academic predicaments that her poor judgment leads to will not help her use the consequences of her actions to make better decisions in the future. Hurrying to find a third job for one's daughter, who just lost the second job in a row because of insubordination to her managers, just so she can keep up with her share of the car insurance is not as helpful as letting the daughter experience the trouble of finding new work herself or face losing the privileges of using the car. The parent may help her scour the want ads, find an employment agency, or practice her interviewing skills, but calling Uncle Lou and getting her tucked away in a position where her work attitude will not be challenged won't help this girl develop the skills she needs to function independently as a young adult.

## How Parents Can Compromise a Child's or Adolescent's Developing Sense of Responsibility

### ▣ *Confusing excessive leniency for fostering creativity*

"I didn't want to compromise my child's creativity by imposing a lot of rules on her so young," says a mother of a fourteen-year-old girl who rules the roost with her temper, "but I'm afraid I've raised a little monster instead!"

Creativity does not come from freedom. It comes from self-confidence and the pleasure of knowing you can make something happen. The most creative children are those who have the self-discipline to organize their creative thoughts, make an innovative plan, and follow it to fruition. Children who grow up in lax homes don't develop the necessary skills to shape and manifest the creativity they might otherwise have.

■ *Confusing gratuitous affirmations and liberties for self-esteem-building*

Dousing children with hollow compliments that don't reflect anything about their inner being—*their person*—does nothing to build self-esteem. Self-esteem comes from people feeling competent in the tasks expected of them, worthy of respect and regard from others, and genuinely likeable. Helping a child become the type of person who feels this way about himself comes from consistently (but not constantly) shaping their actions and responses in interpersonal settings; modeling pro-social behaviors and attitudes; demonstrating compassion, tolerance, and generosity under all of life's circumstances; and repeatedly discussing why these qualities are desirable and admirable. These activities, *done together as a family,* lead children to feel very good about themselves and the kind of person they are growing up to be. There's no better gift for self-esteem than that.

■ *Trying to make up for traumas, tragedies, or losses in a child's past by not addressing current problems*

Sad as they may have been, a small child's tragedies can't be undone by soft parenting. It does the little one no good to grow up overindulged or disrespectful of others' rights and feelings. It certainly doesn't make her pain any less, and more than likely it will allow her to become the type of child others don't care to be around. What kind of favor is that? Parenting firmly and parenting compassionately are not exclusive of one another. Despite their proclamations to the contrary, kids and teenagers really rely on a certain degree of structure and monitering to feel safe and secure and worthy of being taught right from wrong.

"But my child has been through so much already (divorce, loss, medical problems), I just don't want to do anything else that will make her feel bad," says a young and battle-worn divorcée sitting before me.

"Helping your daughter grow up to be kind, considerate, responsible, and comfortable relating genuinely and closely with other people is the best thing you can do to avoid her ever feeling badly about herself or her family," I try to reassure her. "Allowing her to think she can whine, pout, or otherwise coerce attention is no gift at all, will never diminish the pain of this family's sad breakup, and will only increase the chances of her being an unhappy girl who won't respect the teenager she will become."

▣ *Making excuses for the teenager's lack of diligence, responsibility, or follow-through*

"He's got such a low opinion of himself already, I worry about making him feel worse," says the father of fourteen-year-old Sammy, who annoys everyone with his offensive, clownish behavior. "So I generally don't say anything to him when he acts this way, although I'll tell you, it drives us all crazy."

I told Sammy's dad that he wasn't doing his son any favors by letting him act the fool and alienate people. I explained that what Sammy needed from his dad was not begrudging complicity, but several quiet talks over a few weeks about how he sees him struggle to get people's attention and company, and how he's worried that he's doing it in a way that makes people feel badly about themselves. Sammy's dad needed to help him see the benevolence and caring in his words more than the criticism, so that Sammy could use the information to change how he related to peers and adults. That, I said to the father, would be an exquisite way for him to help his young son learn to act in ways that enhanced his self-image and self-respect.

Parents will often veer in the direction of overaccommo-dation when they feel badly about the personal problems their teenager is going through. What they aren't realizing, how-ever, is that the lowered expectations actually make matters worse for the teen by sending a message of no confidence. Letting a kid repeatedly blow off his responsibilities out of sympathy doesn't teach him that he can manage his troubles and still function competently—a valuable lesson to take into adulthood. The unconfident, depressed, or socially inept ado-lescent does much better when his parents show faith in his ultimate ability to succeed and provide constructive, sympa-thetic support while still holding him accountable for doing whatever it is he is supposed to be doing (being a decent stu-dent, being a contributing member of the family, being on time to important events, and the like).

# 5

# HELPING THE TEENAGER
# ASSUME RESPONSIBILITY

*Every day, fourteen-year-old Eric "forgets" to walk the dog after he comes home from school. He also needs to be reminded to feed the poor animal in the evening and to bring in the trash cans on Tuesdays and Fridays. He does, however, manage to remember when his favorite television program is on and his most recent video game score. Nonetheless, Eric's parents go through the daily routine of reminding him to walk the dog, feed the dog, and bring in the cans. They are annoyed to no end but don't know what to do to get him to remember the things they want him to remember.*

*I ask Eric's parents how they handle things when he doesn't follow through on his responsibilities. They look at each other and shrug, then look at me and tell me that they're pretty good about following through on consequences on their end, most of the time, usually, kind of . . . I ask them who cleans up the doggy pee when Eric gets lost in his video games. "Uh, it winds up taking him so long that one of us usually just does it," said Mom.*

*"Not anymore," I replied.*

## The Responsibility Battle

Many teenagers are very good at getting their parents to be the motor behind the actions they should be doing but don't feel like doing. Many parents are good at letting themselves get conscripted into service: *If I don't keep reminding him it doesn't get done. . . .* or, *If I don't sit down with him and actually watch him practice it doesn't happen. . . .* or, *I need to get him up every morning myself because if he uses an alarm clock he just turns it off and goes back to sleep. . . .*

Parents who aren't willing to let their teenager incur a problem or perform at a lower level of academic/social/musical/athletic functioning than they are capable of are at risk for trying to protect their youngster from his or her lapses in diligence, attention, effort, or accountability. Because it's become more important to the parent than to the teenager that the *good/proper/expected/optimal* thing occurs, the parent is vulnerable to working harder than the teen—and harder than the parent really ever should—to make that correct thing happen. What can happen then is that the kid settles in for an easy ride while Mom or Dad starts feeling like a border collie, shepherding their charge through chores, homework, and the day.

---

**The impact of a teenager's choices must always matter more to her than to her parents, or the parents will feel held hostage to needing to make their daughter change her way of thinking and acting.**

---

As long as it is more important to Peggy than to her daughter, Samantha, that Samantha curb her sarcasm and verbal belligerence when in the company of relatives, Peggy is going to dread family reunions. If the prospect of making a scene doesn't bother Samantha, then Peggy needs to impose a consequence for making a scene that would bother Samantha enough to make her consider altering her behavior. Parents who are at the mercy of their child's whim (or, in such a case as this, her propensity for drama) spend too much of their time and energy wondering whether their kid will or won't behave appropriately. Unfortunately, once a teen is willing to frankly defy her parent's directive, the parent has little control over her actions. A parent *can* control the consequences though—what privileges are lost if they proceed to act out in spite of a parent's redirections and/or what privileges are reinstated if they refrain. A parent can't make her daughter *want* to behave appropriately or get good grades or stop smoking cigarettes, but she can use the teenager's wish not to get grounded or have athletic privileges suspended or totally lose her parent's approval to influence her daughter's choices. It's not a home run, but it is a base hit. Sometimes that's all a defiant teen can deliver in the beginning process of change.

---

**It's important for a parent to differentiate between a kid who won't and a kid who can't.**

---

A kid who won't is simply saying no. A kid who can't is suffering from either disabling depression, anxiety attacks, severe learning disabilities, or some other psychological condition that compromises the teenager's ability to function in his day-to-day activities. Feeling on edge about being in the school environment doesn't mean you can't make it through the school day, but a kid who is panic-stricken and experiencing heart palpitations and dizziness at the thought of entering a classroom needs some kind of intervention. Family and/or individual therapy may help, as might medication. Both types of kids need their parents' help, but the kid who can't needs someone to help him figure out how he can, while the kid who won't needs someone to determine, and then let him know, how the outcomes of his choices can (and will) affect him more than they are affecting others. Consultation with a good adolescent and family therapist can be useful to parents who are wondering which kind of teenager they have.

Alex is allergic to grass and pollen, so he can't mow the lawn. But his idea to swap heavy weekend chores with his older, non-allergic brother says a lot about his good intentions. Rob has struggled with reading since the first grade, but his willingness to get tutoring and seek out extra help at school makes it easier for his parents to relax the parameters for acceptable grades.

On the other hand, Mason's recalcitrance about lawn-mowing and his complaints about not having the time to do it hold little water with his parents, who see him spend hours laying around on Saturdays before heading out to meet up with friends in midafternoon. *Plan better,* his parents need to say.

So Mason's parents say that to him the next time he tries to get out of mowing the lawn.

"But stuff just came up, and I'm supposed to pick Julio and Jay up in twenty minutes."

"Sorry, Mason. You're going to have to do a better job of planning your time so that you're free to get up and go when you get the call. But Mom and I are not going to get stuck with your job just because you wanted to sleep in."

"I'll do it tomorrow."

"Tomorrow's not good, Mason. I like the lawn done for the weekend, not after it's over. We go through this every week. *You need to get a better system.*"

Kelly can tell her parents as many times as she wants that her teachers are too busy to help her understand the new material being taught in class, but it remains her responsibility to get her homework assignments done.

"It's not my fault," Kelly whines repeatedly.

"It may not be your fault, but it is your responsibility. I don't hear you talking about staying after school to get help; I don't hear you talking about setting up a meeting with your teachers; I don't hear you asking Dad and me what else you can do; I don't hear you taking any initiative at all. I hear you saying that there's nothing else to do and that it's your teachers' fault because they're busy. I can't buy that. I'm sure they'd make themselves available if they felt you were sincere in your efforts. And so would we."

---

**It's up to a teenager's parents to provide opportunities for the teenager to meet his or her responsibilities, *but it remains the teen's job to make sure that happens.***

---

This is not hands-off parenting. It is parenting that mobilizes. Eric is not reminded to walk the dog every afternoon but instead encouraged to make up a chore checklist that he can work off of independently when he gets home from school. If he still forgets about Rover, he cleans up the pee. Jennifer's parents do not drive her homework sheet over to the school for the umpteenth time when they see it on the kitchen table, but instead ask her if she'd like a special filing box by the back door in which she can put all "outgoing" papers. If she declines the box or still manages to leave her homework at home, she is on her own to handle the situation with her teacher and the consequences of an unsatisfactory report card. Miguel must explain to his boss that he is no longer available to work overtime because he's lost car privileges and now has to coordinate rides with his working parents. His parents guarantee only that they'll get him there for his regular shift, but do not change their schedules just so Miguel can avoid the embarrassment of telling his employer that he messed up.

---

**Kids wishing to avoid responsibility will try to engage parents in emotional discussions in which the parents become more frustrated than the kids do. Thus, the focus shifts from the teenager's noncompliance to the parents' growing irritation and impatience. Suddenly, the parents' reaction is in the spotlight—not the kid's behavior.**

---

Crafty teenagers will dispute facts, challenge a parent's judgment, argue fairness, or attack the quality of their mom's or dad's parenting. The parent who tries to convince his teenager that he's mistaken in his impressions has just bitten the bait: The kid isn't interested in the truth, he's interested in discrediting the parent. Matter-of-fact responses to a teenager's provocations are more effective in keeping attentions where they should be and avoiding a spurious argument.

Matter-of-fact doesn't mean emotionless, however. People who have difficulty blending their reasoning and their emotions often end up exhibiting one side of their point or the other. They come off either as too logical or, alternatively, too dramatic, and lose the kid's attention. Speaking from the heart—be it with frustration, worry, sadness, or humor—can be part of a parent's straightforward response to their adolescent's provocations without their candor or emotions becoming the new focus of attention in the interaction.

For example:

"You are impossibly old-fashioned. Have you realized yet that it's the twenty-first century?" asks fifteen-year-old Alicia.

"Yes," responds her mom.

"Well, you can't really mean I have to dress up to go to that concert."

"Yes, I do mean it."

"I can't believe you!"

"This isn't a rock concert, Alicia. It's a symphony concert. And you need to recognize the difference. That you are making such a fuss about this tells me that you don't. Please go change."

"Ugh!"

Here the parent offers a simple and clear explanation and plainly asserts her stipulation that her daughter dress appropriately for the evening's event. She doesn't allow Alicia's resistance to put her on the defensive, nor does she let it draw them into a battle of whose music is "better," an easy distraction from the real matter at hand. The mother doesn't shy away from showing her sentiments about the situation, but she doesn't make that the focus of her remarks.

Here is another example of adept management on the part of a father of a sixteen-year-old boy who is trying to use his dad's limit-setting as an excuse for having blown off studying for an exam:

> "It's your fault that I failed that test today. If you had let me go out last night as I'd wanted to, I would have been able to study when I got home and done fine. Instead, I was so angry I couldn't even look at a book!" declares Jamey.
>
> "Jamey, you chose to blow off your science test. You handled your anger poorly by having a hissy fit rather than doing what you needed to do in spite of the fact that you were mad at me for saying no to you."
>
> "What I needed was to go out," the boy replies.
>
> "Well, you couldn't. And I'm sorry that you continue to see so many of your problems as being caused by someone else. I hope that changes for you one day. I'm worried you'll end up a bitter old man who thinks he didn't accomplish what he wanted to in life because nobody let him."

The father was wise to keep the argument from dissolving into a heated battle over who was truly responsible for Jamey's failure to study. Trying to "convince" Jamey that he had chosen to have a silent tantrum instead of studying, rather than stating it as an opinion as the father did, would have only fueled the boy's strident disavowals of responsibility. At that moment Jamey wasn't open to being enlightened, and I'm not convinced he needed it. Many times, kids like Jamey know which end is up but manage to convince their parents that they don't. The parents then spend an inordinate amount of time persuading their teenager to consent to a reality the teenager already knows, deep down, to be true.

Jamey's father also avoided lecturing to his son. He didn't tell Jamey that he "needed to become more responsible about his choices." The suggestion is implicit in the discussion, but the change is never mandated. He only pointed out what he saw as having transpired and what he saw as the ultimate consequence of Jamey's refusal to assume responsibility for his actions. It's easier for many teenagers to consider alternative ways of handling things when they don't feel they are doing it in subjugation to an authority figure's demand. For changes that typically evolve over time, such as changes in attitude or perspective, this nonmandated approach works well. Firm expectations of change are better suited to behaviors that are more under a person's voluntary control. A person cannot will himself to *want* to study and do well in school, but he can be expected to spend a decent amount of time in front of his books.

★   ★   ★

HERE is another example that contrasts constructive and destructive handling of a volatile issue:

"I'm going to live with Dad! Your rules are too ridiculous!"

"They may be."

"Well, if you think they're so ridiculous, why don't you change them then?"

"Because I don't mind that they might be ridiculous. You do. Whatever they are, they're my rules and I like them. I'm sorry you don't."

Where *could* that have gone?

"I can't stand it here with all your stupid rules. I'm going to live with Dad."

"Why would you want to do that? Dad's rules are even stricter."

"Oh that's what you think. You don't even know all the things he lets me do."

"I'm well aware of how you spend your time when you are at Dad's house."

"No, you're not. You think you know everything. Dad doesn't make me do any of the stuff you do, and I still get to go out as much as I please."

"You always complain when you come back from Dad's house that he wouldn't let you do anything."

"I don't complain. I love it over there. At least he doesn't treat me like I'm five years old."

"Well, if you wouldn't act five years old, then I wouldn't have to treat you that way."

"You are so mean! Just forget it!"

PUTTING these principles into practice isn't complicated, but it might feel *emotionally* taxing to parents who will need to change how they typically interact with their adolescent children. Sometimes parents will need to say something different. Sometimes they will need to do something different. Effective parenting of teenagers comes in all different forms and can be serious as well as funny. Following are some *strategies that will help parents not address her teenager's problems in ways that cripple the adolescent's interpersonal and problem-solving skills and leave Mom or Dad holding the bag.*

■ *The "this is going to have to be more embarrassing for you than for me" Strategy*

As long as the parent is more inconvenienced or embarrassed by a problem than the teenager is, the teen will have less motivation than the parent to change his inappropriate ways. Parents wanting change more than the kid always are at a disadvantage, and the trick is in turning that around. Here's how Consuelo and George did it with their son, Oscar.

Thirteen-year-old Oscar loved video arcades. He loved them so much he never wanted to leave. Because his family frequently spent time in the mall, finding arcades was no problem. The problem was getting Oscar out of the arcade and into the car.

George and Consuelo had been doing what any reasonable parent might try: They gave five-minute warnings, they threatened loss of privileges, and they got angry—to no avail. Oscar would put his parents off for a few minutes, win yet another free game, and then talk his parents into letting him finish that one, too.

"Have you gone in there and stood right next to him when he's pulled these shenanigans?" I asked Oscar's parents. "Thirteen-year-olds lose their enthusiasm for the game when their parents play cheerleader with all their friends watching."

"Well, no, we hate to make any kind of scene in public, plus, he has such a hard time making friends we didn't want to do anything that would get him teased," they replied.

"He's clever, your Oscar. *He has you guys protecting him from the consequences of his ignoring you.* When is that supposed to become his responsibility? Next time Oscar ignores your request to leave the arcade, walk over to him and whisper in his ear: *'Listen up, love, I'm returning in three minutes to pick you up. If you're not ready, I'm prepared to walk over to where you're standing and give you the biggest hug and kiss you've gotten from me in your life. I promise!'* Then leave."

On the next mall trip, Consuelo and George followed my instructions. Because Oscar feared his parents' public display of affection more than he wanted those free games, he made it out of there in one, not three, minutes. He was taking no chances.

By breaking out of their customary (and ineffectual) strategy of pleading and appeasing, and by doing something completely different, George and Consuelo got Oscar's attention. They also made their point that they would no longer allow themselves to be intimidated by the possibility of their feeling embarrassed in public, or of their son feeling embarrassed. Yet they never needed to resort to being dictatorial in an off-putting or controlling manner. They simply said that when they say it's time to go, it's time to go and that any consequences of Oscar choosing *not* to go were going to fall squarely on him, not them. Moreover, they found a way to keep a sense of humor about the situation.

FOURTEEN-YEAR-OLD Simon had developed a bad habit. Whenever he came home from a Friday evening out with his friends, he asked his parents if one or two of them could spend the night. He knew that his parents had asked him to make any requests for sleepovers the day before and that there were to be no more than one sleepover every two weeks. But, not wanting to embarrass Simon or do something that would start an argument in front of Simon's friends, Lena and Frank would concede. They would then spend the rest of the evening holed away in their room, avoiding the belching bevy of soda-swigging, chip-chomping boys downstairs in the family room.

"Why do you guys say yes to him?" I asked. "You know he knows better than to be asking."

"I'd hate to say no when he has his friends right there," said Lena. "It's an awkward situation. Plus, to tell you the truth, I hate the prospect of spending the evening with him after I've said no. You don't know how obnoxious he can get. It's not worth it."

I told them that they were paying too steep a price to have an easy evening. I added, "He knows you'll feel bad about sending his friends home in front of them, and that's where he has you over a barrel. It matters more to you than to him that they would be sent home and that he would feel embarrassed. The next time Simon asks you to let them stay over, send them home with a casual apology for Simon's putting everyone in such an awkward position. I doubt Simon will try that trick again. Don't let him get away with acting surprised, either. He knows what the expected response is."

"What about all the scowls and howls the rest of the evening?" asked Frank.

"I'd tell him that if he's going to carry on like that on the heels of getting turned down, he can forget about *any* friends staying over for a long time. Tell him you won't put up with it. Then don't. If he continues, ask him to leave the room. If he refuses to leave, tell him that he's just lost the privilege of asking for sleepovers for the next month. Let him storm off. It'll all tone down once Simon gets used to you meaning business."

Lena and Frank looked at each other as if this would be one of the larger challenges they'd faced with their son. Parents whose family routines get organized around avoiding confrontation with a volatile teenager have some difficulties reversing the trend. They fear the backlash from a youngster who has become accustomed to wielding power through his volatility and inflexibility. The backlashes can get punishing, but never as oppressive as having to be miserable or feel restricted in one's own home.

Lena and Frank followed my advice one Friday evening, much to Simon's surprise. They declined his request for two friends to stay the night and politely asked the boys to call for their rides home. Simon, making himself believe they were joking, ignored his parents and suggested to his friends that they do the same. Made self-conscious and uncomfortable by Simon's behavior, the two boys got up to make their calls. Simon had a tantrum, calling his parents "rude" and "inconsiderate" and "poor models for how to treat guests." Simon's friends tried to get him to calm down, telling him it was no big deal, but Simon assumed a moral outrage of embarrassing proportions. His friends finally left, and Simon finally settled down. He blamed Lena and Frank for what he worried his friends would now be saying about him and his uptight parents.

Simon tried it one more time, two weeks later. This time, as soon as Lena and Frank mentioned to Simon that he had offered no advance notice, Simon's friends apologized to his parents and headed to the phone to call for rides home. When Simon protested that his parents were "mistreating" his guests, one of his friends said the only one mistreating anyone was Simon himself, who was acting like a jerk. "Knock it off, Simon. This is getting old," his friend said before leaving the house to wait outside for his ride. The other boy followed suit.

Simon waited a long time before asking his parents if another friend could stay over. But when he did, he asked a week in advance. He still acted as if he were the host of all hosts and positioned on a higher moral ground than his parents, who previously had so "coldly" turned his friends away, but Lena, Frank, and I were convinced he knew better. When your own friends agree with your parents instead of with you, it's time to change your tune.

### ▣ Don't take the fall for the teenager's poor choices

Every morning the Land home is controlled by the choices and actions of fourteen-year-old Samantha. She stays in bed until both her mom and dad have threatened to ground her for the rest of the day unless she comes down to breakfast in five minutes. Five minutes later she has another five minutes to come down. Five minutes later she still has three minutes left to go. When she hears her mom stomping up the stairs, she gets out of bed and yells, *"I'm coming already! Give me a break."*

In the kitchen, Dad is racing around to feed Samantha's two brothers, and Mom is gulping some breakfast in anticipation of Samantha's missing the bus and needing to be driven to school once again. Dad, Mom, and Samantha's brothers are angry. Samantha is indifferent. She saunters down the stairs and asks what's for breakfast.

"London broil," remarks one of her brothers, sarcastically. "Dad had time to cook it while we were all waiting for you to decide to get out of bed."

"Oh, like you don't ever sleep in."

"At least I do it on my own time."

"I'm bothering you? You look like you've had time to shovel enough cereal into your mouth this morning to keep you happy. Mind your own business."

"We would, but it's hard when you make such a scene."

Samantha rolls her eyes and butters a slice of bread. She

tries to look as if she's hurrying up, but it's obvious to everyone that once again she will allow herself to miss her bus. Her mother will drive her to school because her mother is more concerned about Samantha being late than Samantha is. Samantha's mom will show up approximately forty-five minutes late for work, again.

I ask Samantha's mom why she continues to take the hit for Samantha's dawdling.

"It's so far to walk. And then she'd get in so late, and possibly even miss her entire first period. I don't know what else to do. I feel like I have no choice but to drive her."

"You have choices. Here's what I'd suggest. If you feel like it's reasonable for Samantha to walk to school, tell her that as of tomorrow you'll no longer be available to drive her. Explain that you were so worried about her doing well at school that it made you do things that aren't going to help her in the long run, like bailing her out when she lets herself be late. Tell her that she's a big girl and she can get up after your first—and only—wake-up call and get herself to school. If she's late, she's late, and she'll have to deal with whatever consequences her school administration imposes, as well as the ones that you and her dad set up for getting late notices. If it's not reasonable for her to walk to school, explain to her that whatever amount of time she takes away from your plans for the day by having to be driven to school are to be "paid back" at twice the rate. If taking her to school causes you to lose forty-five minutes, Samantha owes you an hour and a half of chore time. She makes the choice."

"But what if she's late a lot?" Samantha's mom asks.

"Then she's late a lot. Let your daughter be late and have

to deal with it. Impose consequences so that getting up on time and making the bus wind up being less of a hassle to her than getting to school in the middle of first period. If she's late, she can't use the phone that day, for example. If she's home from school before anyone else and you don't trust her to lay off the phone, unplug them all and take them with you. Make your point that you are willing to be inconvenienced in ways that *you* choose in order to avoid being inconvenienced in ways that are chosen for you by her. If Samantha is like most teenagers, this won't take long to resolve."

At first Samantha complained furiously to her parents that they were just doing whatever some "shrink" told them to do and that it was stupid. She claimed that they didn't care about her schooling, and she couldn't believe they wouldn't at least continue to wake her up in the morning, *after all* what was the big deal? Then she simply got herself down to breakfast and on the bus. She was miserable to share the breakfast table with for the first few weeks, but most of that was probably for show, just to make sure everyone knew how offended she was by the whole thing and how much she didn't like it. Her brothers teased her mercilessly for her timely departures but were relieved to no end by the evaporating morning arguments.

▣ *Get Out of the Middle*

There are many ways in which parents overaccommodate their teenager's irresponsible behavior. Confusing protection from the natural consequences of their child's behavior for benevolent support, these parents wind up doing a great dis-service to their child by repeatedly bailing them out. Consider the efforts of Roberta's parents to keep her from ever going hungry—they picked up the lunch she regularly left on the kitchen table and brought it to her high school when she was a sophomore.

"She gets so cranky when she doesn't eat, and I want her to have a fresh mind for her studies," her mom offered as an excuse.

"I can't believe she even *lets* you bring her lunch," I responded.

"Oh, yes, she'll call me on her cell phone from school and tell me she's starting to shake she's so hungry and ask if I could please bring her lunch over. What can I do?"

"Let her go hungry once or twice, and let her *friends* be the ones to tell her she's too cranky. She might just get the point," I suggested.

"But she'll start blaming me for feeling sick or doing poorly in her afternoon classes."

"Martha, that's bogus. You know it, and I know it, but most important, Roberta knows it. Don't validate her accusation by taking it seriously. Instead, just smile at her through the phone and tell her you think you've been making a mistake all these years rescuing her and that you think all you've managed to do is help her become a 'good forgetter.' She'll roll her eyes, hang up the phone, and find something to eat off a friend to hold her through the day. The next day she'll bring her lunch."

I was wrong. It took two days of going without lunch for Roberta to cure her forgetfulness. How? It was quite simple.

She put her lunch in her backpack instead of on the kitchen table.

### ▣ *Abandon efforts to stay "rational" in favor of getting "real"*

Parents' efforts to get an irrational teenager to become more rational by acting more rational themselves usually accomplish two things: The teen gets more irrational, and the parents get angrier. The problem is that a teen can easily construe his parents' attempts to inject reason into the conversation as an attempt to "control" their emotions by pointing out mistakes in their thinking. Sometimes, the best road out of that imbroglio is to revert to simpler matters of the heart. A parent's candor about his difficulty reaching the adolescent can often affect the teen much more powerfully than any discussion about "being rational."

Mack, father of thirteen-year-old Gregory, sat in my office looking for help in better managing his son's outrageous and abusive verbal attacks on him and his wife, Wendy.

"When he starts to go off, I try to get him to calm down," Mack explains to me. "It just doesn't work."

"What do you say?" I ask.

"I try to stay very calm, cool, and collected and tell Greg that he's beginning to get upset and that he should stop now in order to control himself."

"How does Greg respond to that?"

"By getting even more in my face and telling me that I can't control him anymore."

Mack wasn't aware how poorly kids typically respond to being told to "calm down" by their parents. They experience this as the parent staying *out of the relationship*; it feels aloof, lecture-ish, and patronizing. Parents need to protect themselves from their teenager's ranting but also address their difficulty appreciating the point the teen is trying to express. They can try saying something like *I don't like what you're doing, and it makes it hard for me to stay connected to you when you do that.*

"Mack, the next time Greg gets fired up, try saying something like the following. I think he may be able to respond to it better than to your requests that he calm down. *'Look, Greg, this conversation is going in an ugly direction. It's too bad, because I don't want to argue, but it's looking pretty bleak right now. I had wanted us to enjoy each other's company tonight, but I'm having trouble listening to your side of things right now. Maybe we'll try again tomorrow. The answer to your question about using the car this afternoon is still no, by the way.'*"

This response accomplishes several things.

**First,** it communicates a commitment to the relationship coupled with self-respect—the father won't make himself available to abusive dialogues. Note that the father never has to use the word *abusive*, which would be incendiary and likely to provoke a defensive posture on the adolescent's part. It is implied instead.

**Second,** the response is firm without being gruff or rigidly authoritarian and says, essentially, that the father is going to pull the plug on the discussion, not because he doesn't want to talk, but because it's unlikely to be productive.

**Third,** there is emotion in the father's response. It's not aloof and "overly rational." It has some heart in it, and the adolescent can feel like he is engaging with a person who is

not so busy trying to avoid getting upset that he can't be a little vulnerable himself.

**Fourth,** the statement is forthright and candid. Few emotions affect other human beings in a relationship as poignantly as
candor. It is simultaneously arresting, expressive, personal, honest, and inviting. It often comes as a surprise, and it is usually very
disarming. I find that people will become much less defensive
when the other person with whom they are arguing uses candor in talking about their experience with the problem at hand.

Candor doesn't involve making casual or provocative remarks to the teenager, nor is it an excuse to speak unkindly.
It's not an excuse to "let fly" with whatever is going on in a
parent's mind, and it's never an excuse for power plays. The
kind of candor that prompts an adolescent to consider
thoughtfully what his parent is saying and take it to heart is a
benevolent frankness that invites that boy to look at himself
differently—*but without containing any injunction for the teen to
change*; for example:

> . . . I wish we could manage to get through one of these
> discussions without always storming off to our rooms; it actu-
> ally leaves me feeling more sad than angry. . . .

> . . . You talk about being moody and miserable as if it were
> your shoe size and there was nothing you could do about it.
> It's like you've just resigned yourself, and that bothers me. It
> worries me, too.

> . . . Do you know that sometimes I think that if I were a
> better parent I would somehow know how to keep us from

arguing so much? But then at other times I just think that you won't let yourself trust me to be on your side. *I'm on your side.*

In Mack's situation, the response I suggested allows Greg to hear not just more complaints about his bad behavior but also his father's interest in having had more contact that evening and a better resolution to the problem. Without becoming solicitous or too accommodating with his son, Mack has made the problem *their* problem and not just Greg's problem. However, the problem is still framed as one for which Greg has full accountability.

# 6

## HELPING KIDS SAVE FACE

Betty and Arthur couldn't understand why their eighteen-year-old son was continuing to skip so many of his senior high school classes and disregard the majority of his assignments. It didn't make any sense—Kyle was intelligent, sociable, and industrious. On his own, he'd spend hours designing and completing projects in his makeshift workshop in the garage. But let his science teacher assign a similar project, and Kyle wasn't interested. He'd let the deadline come and go without a second thought.

"It's not logical!" Kyle's dad exclaimed in my office during their first visit. "He'll stay up all hours for some project of his own and sometimes even pass on going out with friends for the sake of finishing some part of it. But let Betty and me threaten to ground him from going out for not completing one of his science or language projects, and we have hell to pay from him all weekend long. It's ridiculous."

Well, it *doesn't* make sense, but there is another type of logic operating here. I call it emotional logic. Emotional logic is a combination of a person's beliefs, attitudes, and life experiences that are filtered through his personality, and it has an enormous effect on how that person will react to the events in his life. Emotional logic is what has us say no when we really want to say yes, what has us indulge an impulsive decision rather than stay patient, and what has us stubbornly persist with something even though we know it doesn't work. We do these things for what we think at the time are *good* reasons, even if they aren't *smart* reasons. Sometimes, we'd rather be right than smart.

So it is with teenagers. Sometimes—many times— teenagers will make an unwitting choice to be right (at least in their own mind) rather than admit to what would feel like defeat or overdependence or overcompliance. So they make bad choices and live with them, while everyone else stands around scratching their heads, wondering about the illogic of it all. It's their way of saving face.

Parents of adolescents often feel stumped by an invisible but apparent rigidity in their child's thinking. It feels to them as if their teen is being stubborn, argumentative, immature, or belligerent. The teen only knows that he or she doesn't want to or can't do something that everyone wants them to do.

Conflicts between parents and teens arise from the inevitable clash of perceptions and "logical" assumptions. These conflicts are hard to resolve at the manifest level. The good news, however, is that teenagers will often soften their beliefs or position once they feel their parents appreciate their perspective, even if they disagree with it. It's amazing how flexible the teen, who, only moments before was irascibly defiant, can become once the meaning of the fight is understood.

Following are five common adolescent beliefs that underlie many of the rigid positions they adopt in relation to the responsibilities they are being asked by parents, teachers, and employers to assume. They are adopted not to fight or alienate, but rather to preserve their fragile sense of dignity and independence. They follow an emotional logic all their own.

1. *"I can't want it (school, being alcohol-free, a job) if I know that you want it, too."*

This is where Kyle was getting stuck. Because his parents and teachers wanted him to do well in school and complete his assignments (as one would expect they would), he felt unable to publicly share in those same goals. Did he want those same things? Sure. But now they were ruined because they'd been contaminated by adult endorsement.

In order for Kyle to take pleasure in his academic accomplishments, he had to feel as if he were the only one who cared whether or not they got done. That's why he did so well with independent projects in his garage workshop. Even though his parents enjoyed the results of his creativity and industry, it was Kyle's decision alone to initiate the projects. Had his parents started to show more of an interest in Kyle *completing* those projects than he had, he'd have dropped them like a hot potato.

Why did Kyle act in such a self-defeating way? Stubborn? Maybe a little. Irrational? Not entirely, especially when you see things from Kyle's point of view. Feeling that very little in his life was accomplished without it being the directive of a parent, teacher, or other authority figure, Kyle tried to carve out a way to feel that *he* was in charge of something—even if it meant being in charge of it not happening. What is rational about all this is that, based on his premise that *being in charge was more important than succeeding,* Kyle's actions made sense. In order to change his actions and make a wiser decision, Kyle needed to modify his premise.

"But that could take a lot of time," worried Betty and Arthur. "By the time he gets a different attitude, he could fail his courses for the marking period. Isn't there anything else we could do?"

They could sit down with Kyle and explain to him that they think it's hard for him to want something like good grades if he feels that his parents want it for him, too. Nonetheless, they were going to insist on good grades, and if that caused a problem of pride for him, he'd have to work it out in his head so that he felt he could pursue the grades *even if his parents wanted it, too.*

This meant that Kyle had to either override his feeling that he was complying with someone else's requests rather than doing what he wanted to, and do it anyway, or learn that to do something that others wanted him to do wasn't demeaning, even though it might feel that way. The point is that he had to find some way to get the job done, and his parents holding him compassionately but consistently accountable for how he configured his dilemma would help push him toward a solution. The position they needed to take was one of:

*We understand that this is difficult for you because you think that doing something for yourself that someone else also wants for you is kind of like giving in. It doesn't have to be that way, but we know better than to try to convince you otherwise. From our standpoint, though, no matter how you choose to figure things, what we need to*

*see you doing is going to school and getting good grades. If you see*
*some way for us to help you through your dilemma, let us know.*

Kyle's reluctance to commit to things that other people in
his life saw as good for him reminds me of another teenager
whose family I consulted with. Jill, a lively and articulate girl
of fifteen going on twenty-one, began skipping her eleventh-
grade classes. Despite her parents' best efforts to talk to her
about the importance of school and to establish consequences
for her behavior, Anne and Brian were met with irritating,
cavalier quips about education and libertarianism and threats
to drop out of school entirely. What baffled them most, however, was that Jill had always loved school and actually seemed
to miss her friends, school activities, and some of her classes.

In their first therapy session, Anne and Brian realized that
their daughter had inadvertently painted herself into a psychological corner: In spite of her unspoken but apparent
wishes to return to school, Jill felt she couldn't because she
believed that everyone would think she was returning *only be-*
*cause they had told her to do so.* Scolding, imploring with logic
about the need for education, and punishing her through the
removal of her stereo, compact discs, or favorite articles of
clothing—not unreasonable efforts—weren't effective in getting Jill back to school because they served only to further entrench her in her conflict.

Once Jill's parents understood the emotional dilemma their
daughter was in, they were able to approach the problem in a
different way. I told them to do two things. One was to sit
down with Jill and explain to her that they now recognized
her dilemma that if she went back to school, it would never

feel as if it were her idea. The second was to tell her that she had a choice: She either could learn to continue to want something even if grown-ups wanted it for her, too, and return to school, or she could continue on her soapbox, and *they would attend school for her.* This intervention was simultaneously firm, appreciative of the adolescent's psychological position, and encouraged accountability for Jill's actions *in spite of how she felt.* Jill's parents demonstrated empathy for her conflict while still making it clear that she had a responsibility to go to school. Were Jill to have continued to fight her fight, the consequences of having her mom and dad alternately sit at her desk next to her friends at school would have been much harder for her to bear than the inconvenience to Anne and Brian. Jill chose to attend school, and the anguish it caused her became the conversation of our sessions. Now we had something to talk about other than Jill's belief in the merits of laissez-faire educational policies and "adolescent rights."

The cheekiness of this kind of intervention appeals to some families but not all. In a million years, Betty and Arthur, an older and more somber couple, couldn't have imagined themselves sitting in for Kyle in his classes. They wouldn't have needed to, though. Kyle's greater age and maturity compared to Jill, plus his better-developed capacity for self-reflection, meant that he was able to use his parents' remarks and the therapy sessions to get a different perspective on his need to be the only one invested in the outcome of his academic endeavors. He used that different perspective to then make different choices. Jill, on the other hand, less mature and much more cavalier about her lack of attendance and effort, needed the concrete consequence of prospective embarrassment to get herself back to school. Less genuine and less autonomous than the changes Kyle was making, Jill's changes nonetheless accomplished the immediate and urgent goal of preventing her from becoming a real truant.

2. *"As long as I think of an idea as yours it will never feel like mine. I may like it, but I can't use it."*

This face-saving effort is a second cousin to the prior one. What happens here is that the teenager rejects any *idea* that originates in someone else's head—*even ones he believes to be good.* This is what parents sometimes run into when they try to give their kid great advice on a problem that he or she brings to their attention, only to find the advice dismissed out of hand.

"Sherri sat me down on the edge of her bed the other day practically in tears and told me about this argument she was having with her boyfriend," says the sympathetic mother of a seventeen-year-old high school junior. "It all seemed to be a big misunderstanding, so I suggested a few things that she seemed to think were good ideas. She even said so at the time. The next day after school, though, she looked at me as if I were crazy when I asked her if she'd followed any of my advice. She said she really appreciated what I'd said, but she needed to work things out her own way. Go figure."

I told this mother that she probably helped her daughter more than she realized. Maybe Sherri *appeared* to dismiss her advice out of hand, but she very likely did think about it, which is valuable even if she chooses not to act on it—this time. Also, although Sherri may say she's not using the advice, it may have made enough of an impression to have influenced her handling of the problem in some positive way. And the fact that her mother took the time to listen to her problem and try to help surely meant a lot to the daughter (whether she would acknowledge it or not). Often, the specifics of *what* is said are less important than the act of saying something and providing a supportive and stabilizing presence in the adolescent's life.

Sherri reminds me of fifteen-year-old Tina, who I saw for therapy for a variety of problems, including fighting with her parents, skipping school, failing grades, and alcohol use. During one session, Tina and I were talking about how she tends to withdraw from her friends, family, and other potential support figures whenever her problems become acute.

"Of all times, why then?" I asked Tina. "Why do you pull away from the people who most could help you and would want to help you?"

"Because unless I solve my problems by myself, *it won't count*," replied this sad, lonely girl who had mixed up what it means to be a kid and what it means to be independent.

"Won't count for what?" I asked.

"For anything. If someone helps me get over some problem, then I really didn't do it, so it's not really solved. So then it might even come back, and that would be worse because I'd have thought it was done with. So I just try and figure out problems myself."

"Is it working?" I wondered out loud.

"Not really. I mean, at least not yet. But I'll be able to do it. Tomorrow I'm going to stay in school all day. And, like, I'm not going to argue with my mom anymore anyway, because it's no use, so I think I'm okay."

Tina's attempts to solve her problems by herself were not good ones. Naïve and immature, they left her back at square one within a day or two, sometimes within hours of her proposed "solutions." Without the guidance of her parents, counselors, or even her friends, she was sinking further into depression and desperation.

I told Tina that, in part, I greatly respected her attempts to solve her problems on her own. It showed her wish to be self-reliant and thorough—traits that would serve her well in a lot of areas in her life, but not in the ones she was wrestling with right now. I said she had a little too much of the old American frontiersman spirit in her and that this was a good time for her to learn one of the other lessons that the frontier taught—that in order to survive, people need a community.

Parents of a kid like Sherri or Tina can do something similar. They can talk to their "individualist" child about the need for balance in everything in life, including individualism. They can let her know that although they respect their child's efforts to solve her own problems, it takes nothing away from a person to accept a little help. Examples from the parent's own life, or from the lives of other loved or admired figures (grandparents, family friends, public role models) of accepting help, perhaps after failed attempts at some problem or endeavor, would add color and impact to the conversation and help the teenager realize that she is not the only one who (erroneously) has ever thought it best to take care of matters by herself.

3. *"I will stop acting up as soon as you stop watching and waiting for me to change my behavior."*

Few things inhibit a teenager from changing her behavior

more than thinking her parents are looking over her shoulder, waiting for that first indication that she's doing things differently. Parents anticipating or hoping for changes in behavior or attitude get better results when they give their teenager some space to begin handling things differently. Depending on the nature and urgency of the problem, the "space" could be anything from a few minutes to a few days. Some kinds of attitude-shifts happen gradually over a course of a few weeks and are decelerated by the teen if parents nag, remind, or ask about it. Keeping the spotlight off the teenager allows her to feel as if she has some control over the timing and circumstances of change and diminishes her resistance to doing what she was asked or told to do. Taking initiatives to apologize, relating more straightforwardly, taking school more seriously, and other general behaviors and attitudes are the kinds of things that may take a little while for the adolescent to put into full effect. They are very different from the kinds of changes that parents of difficult-to-manage teens are entitled to see immediately effected. Examples of this would be returning home by curfew, speaking respectfully to others, respecting family members' privacy, getting to school on time, refraining from prohibited activities, and other similar behaviors where margins of tolerance are narrower.

Many parents inadvertently inhibit changes their child was in the process of making by putting too fine a spotlight on the rate of progress—or lack thereof. The teen, feeling self-conscious and scrutinized, pulls back and either discontinues what she had been doing or proceeds in ways that she is sure will not be apparent to her parents.

Choosing not to acknowledge a kid's progress is tricky,

though, because some kids *love* the fact that a parent notices their efforts to change. A parent needs to know which kid he or she has—one who wants the accolades or one who doesn't. Applaud the wrong kind of teenager and you get the following, as articulated by a sixteen-year-old boy whose parents were concerned about his diminishing interest in school and his argumentative and disrespectful attitude toward family members:

"Look, I know I've been a pain in the rear to everybody," Todd told me in a private session. "I don't really mean to be. But whenever I start to act more like what they want, my folks start congratulating me like I've done this big thing, and I hate it. The way they go on and on makes it sound like they're talking to a six-year-old. Besides, it sounds kind of silly, but, to me, all their congratulating just makes it even more obvious that I've been messing up. I wish they'd just be more cool about the whole thing."

But for a parent with a teenager who *likes* knowing that her efforts are being noticed and appreciated, a parent being cool about the whole thing might seem a little *too* chilly. The kid wanting a little fanfare is left wondering if anyone is even paying attention. If she decides they aren't, she just might forget about it and go back to her old ways, or continue as she had been, but with a big chip on her shoulder.

Parents can determine which kind of teenager they have by being aware of their child's preferences about similar matters and by gauging their responses to small interventions. They can tell whether their child is one who benefits from positive reinforcement about changes he is making or if he sees the reinforcement as patronizing. For instance, when Andrew brings home good work from school, does he enjoy hearing his parents' praise, or does he get embarrassed and try to low-key his accomplishments? Does Rachel enjoy having her mom cheer her on at her soccer games, or does she prefer a more sedate spectator style? When Rashid finally started to feed the dog regularly without being reminded, did he enjoy his parents' gracious thank-yous, or did he dismissively shrug them off? Answering these and similar questions about their adolescent will give parents an accurate sense of how comfortably he tolerates pats on the back and identify the ones who become shy.

Occasionally, a parent of a teenager who is shy about being complimented has trouble holding back from saying something when the inappropriate behavior has stopped or diminished. What can that father say that won't lead to a relapse? The best strategy is for him to be as candid as possible about his dilemma of *wanting to say something because he is so pleased with what's been happening, but thinking he shouldn't because it will make his daughter too self-conscious.* This candor allows the father to express his pleasure without actually *applauding* the teenager in a way that could make her uncomfortable. Parents can even ask the teen what they should do: *"Zach, I've always thought it made you uncomfortable when we make too big a deal about something you've done, so I want to ask you what might seem a funny question. What should Mom and I do when we see you doing such a good job of pulling yourself and your schoolwork together? Should we say something or not?"* When Zach looks over at his dad as if to say, *You're crazy,* his dad shrugs and smiles back.

This style of talking is a great way of creating more genuineness in the relationship. People often choose to not say the things they're thinking because they don't know how to, or they think it will sound silly, or they worry that the conversation will become awkward.

But clumsy, silly, or awkward conversations can be our warmest, funniest, or most intimate. We can trust our teenagers to let them see us being clumsy, silly, or self-conscious not only because it models a genuine way of being, but because it allows us to give up so many of our private thoughts that didn't need to be kept so private in the first place.

**4. *"Sometimes it feels good to see you as confused and out of control as I feel."***

Janine could never understand why her mother's composure in the face of her own tantrums drove her crazy. She couldn't identify, let alone articulate, that it made her mom seem so remote and unreachable. But she could manage to bait her mom into arguments in which her mom would gradually get aggravated and frustrated enough to finally snap back. *Gotcha,* Janine would think, happy again and smug with the knowledge that she was able to break her mother's cool and reduce her—in Janine's eyes—to the level of upset she felt best matched her own.

Parents of a *gotcha* kind of kid can productively deal with the issue by addressing it nonconfrontationally but very directly:

- **Janine's mom can ask her daughter what it is about seeing her blow her cool that so satisfies her.**
  Janine's mother needs to be careful to ask a genuine question and not use the discussion as an opportunity to be

sarcastic or critical of Janine's provocative behavior. If she asks a real question, and communicates a genuine wish to understand, she will likely get a real response:

- *I don't know, Mom. I guess it just makes me feel better to see you upset. It's like I'm not the only one upset anymore.*

- *It's the only time I ever see you not know what to say. You always know exactly what you're going to say, and it's just, I don't know, it's just so in control all the time. I never know what I'm going to say until it comes out of my mouth.*

It would be important for the mother *not* to pounce on Janine's moment of self-reflection and disclosure by saying something like, *"Yes, I know, and that's why you get in trouble all the time."* She needs to consider that her perspective is not the only perspective and instead say, *"Yeah, I can see how I might come across like that. And now that you say that, I don't know that I want to come off as so controlled all the time. It makes me seem so un-spontaneous!"*

- **The mom openly recognizing what had been a covert operation on Janine's part and encouraging tolerance for each other's vulnerabilities.**

"Look, Janine," the mom says, "I know you love to see me go off on you because it makes you feel as if you've 'won' or something. I have trouble keeping calm when you say some of the more outrageous things you can say. I know it, and I try to contain it, but sometimes I just can't. It's my problem, not yours. I just wish you'd not use it as an opportunity to feel victorious, and instead, work with me on genuinely trying to solve whatever problem we're having at that moment. Would you try doing that with me?" Only the angriest and most resentful of kids will spit on that overture; if that were to happen, then Janine's mom can further use her candor and try to alter the decaying state of the relationship:

- *"Whatever has happened to the two of us that you have such contempt for my idea of trying to get along better?"*

- *"Well, look, my offer's on the table, Janine. When you're ready for us to try and move forward, let me know. This is just a very sad and awful situation, and I hate living this way."*

- *"Janine, you just blow me away with how unforgiving and inaccessible you can be sometimes. I don't know how to reach you anymore, and it scares the daylights out of me."*

### 5. *"It's more important for me to feel 'right' than to do the smart thing."*

Many adolescents have chosen to go down with the ship rather than concede defeat.

Emily had known for quite some time that her choice of boyfriend was lousy. Nicky was coarse and coersive, and he fit in poorly with the close group of friends she'd made and kept since her freshman year at high school. A senior now and a strong student, Emily was trying to decide among different colleges, while Nicky unrelentingly would try to get her to cut classes, skip school, and neglect her studies. "C'mon," Nicky would urge, "those stupid applications are in and no one's going to care what you do the rest of the year. Let's go have some fun."

Emily's shine to Nicky had been wearing off since winter break, and she often daydreamed about breaking it off. Her biggest problem, though, was the strident vote of confidence in both Nicky's character and the longevity of their relationship she had made to her skeptical parents when she and Nicky had first started going out. To turn to her parents one morning and say, "Guys, you know, he really is the creep you said he was, and I am breaking it off" would feel to Emily as if she'd hung her pride out to dry. She wouldn't even have to go that far in agreeing with her parents' earlier assessment. Saying only that "they'd broken up" would be enough to make her feel *as if* she were saying, *Okay, guys, you were right, and I was wrong. Nicky's bad news.* So what does this poor girl do? She does what a lot of girls and boys in similar situations do—they stick it out until they think no one's looking, spot an exit, and find some excuse for why it didn't work out that has nothing to do with the original concerns of the parents who predicted it wouldn't work in a million years.

Parents who give their kids a way to save face as they back down, reconsider, change their mind, or otherwise abandon their earlier posts help that child or teenager enormously to not feel as if they need to hang on until the very end. Everyone feels the relief.

Too many teenagers go down in the annals of their family history as having been "impossible," "defiant," or "totally irrational" during their adolescence. Some are, no doubt, but more are not, and many who come off that way to the adults who are raising, educating, and otherwise guiding them may seem so because of their intense needs to feel respected, think and do for themselves, and believe that they have the major hand in orchestrating their lives.

When we give them the benefit of the doubt for their more urgent beliefs (not actions) and try to understand what social or psychological need that teenager is trying to gratify, many of the brewing battles can be averted. Teenagers love being understood and appreciated for what they go through. Helping them express what they need us to do for them and what they don't is a cherishable gift for any parent or mentor to give.

# SECTION TWO

◾

# *Family Stories*

# 7

## ADAM

### Managing the Volatile Adolescent

*"He gets so angry, I can hardly say 'boo.'"*

"When he's in a good mood, he's the greatest kid around, but when he's not happy, he's unbearable," Adam's mom says, describing her fifteen-year-old son to me on the telephone.

"How unbearable?" I ask.

"Well, he gets pretty out of control," Darlene says.

"What will he do?" I ask.

"Well, he's, um, punched a few holes in the wall, destroyed one of his drawers. . . ." Darlene's voice trails off.

"Anything else?"

"Uh, last week I told him he had to do the dinner dishes, and he set the kitchen tablecloth on fire."

We set up a time for Darlene to come in with Adam, and I told her to be sure that Adam's dad, Evan, would be able to come as well. When they arrived, I observed Darlene and Evan twice asking Adam if he wanted a drink of water and if he needed to use the rest room before the session. Adam didn't respond. Instead, he strolled the waiting room floor, looking sullen and disinterested. When Adam accidentally knocked his dad's coat onto the floor, he left it there. Adam watched silently as his dad picked it up while mumbling something under his breath.

Darlene looked over to me from her seat in the waiting room and shrugged as if to say, *See what I mean?* I smiled, but already I was seeing her son differently than she saw him. I saw a kid who was not being held accountable for his rude behavior. I also saw two parents who were bending over backward to avoid a problem. Unfortunately, they already had a problem—one considerably bigger than any argument they were trying to avoid.

When I asked the family how I could be of help, both parents turned to Adam and urged him to begin talking to me. Clearly, they were not taking charge of managing Adam's attitude and behavior problems, but instead they were appealing to what they hoped would be Adam's desire to change how he felt and acted. Unfortunately, he didn't have any such desire. Adam didn't think he needed help, and he saw no need for us to talk. I suggested to Darlene and Evan that they tell me a little more about their concerns for Adam, and I mentioned casually that Adam could speak up if he felt he had something to say. Not allowing Adam's silence and lack of participation to direct the session was a first, important step toward disarming this boy who characteristically tried to wield power by withholding his participation.

Darlene expanded her previous account of the difficulties she and Evan had been having with Adam, and Evan added his perspective. His experiences were similiar to Darlene's—

frequent conflicts over household responsibilities, Adam's treatment of his younger brother, his erratic academic performance, and his lack of adherence to his curfew. Evan acknowledged being terribly uncomfortable with conflict, avoiding it whenever possible. He'd hoped over the past six months that Adam would "come around," grow out of it, or just get tired of fighting.

Adam didn't do any of those things. Instead, his behavior got more extreme, and his attitude more strident. He criticized his parents' principles, made fun of his younger brother whenever he abided by their rules, and distanced himself from the family at holiday dinners and other family functions. The more Darlene and Evan asked Adam to change his ways, the more contemptuous he got. They had reached a point where they feared saying much to him when he was upset, because it would always blow up into an argument so ugly it would hang over the household for days.

I asked Adam's parents about the last time they remembered their family doing well together. They picked a time about a year before, when Adam seemed happier and less reactive. He would seek out Darlene after coming home from school just to touch base for a few minutes. He would also easily accompany Evan on errands and occasionally enjoy bowling or fishing with his dad. There were disagreements and the occasional yelling match, especially between Adam and Evan, but these generally blew over with little residual tension. The demands on Adam were few, his parents noted, and there were even fewer rules. But because Adam wasn't pushing the limits at all, there were few scuffles.

I asked Adam if he agreed with his parents' description of

the problems the family was having. He nodded. I asked if he remembered the time his parents were referring to as having been better. He nodded again but looked away. I asked Darlene and Evan to describe one of their more recent arguments. Evan chose one that had occurred the week before, in which Adam refused to help him repair the back porch.

"I wasn't refusing," snarled Adam, in his first spontaneous contribution to the session.

"Well, you sure weren't jumping up and down when I asked you to give me a hand," Evan replied.

"That's just it!" Adam cried out. "Unless I practically stand to attention and act all excited over some dumb job you want me to do, you think I'm not going to do it!"

"But you *don't* do it, Adam."

"That's because by the time you're done asking and getting on my case for not doing it 'with a smile,' I'm so angry I can't do it! But that doesn't mean I wasn't going to do it or that I was *refusing*." Adam looked off to the side with frustration before resting his head in his hands.

Not wanting to referee so early in the game, I asked Darlene what she does when Evan and Adam argue.

"Oh, I usually try and get them to stop fighting."

"How?"

Evan interceded. "She will typically tell me not to make such an issue of something and to let it drop 'for now.' The only problem is that Adam and I never get back to it—until our next fight about it. I'm left feeling angry at both of them, plus, I then have to do the job myself while Adam goes up to his computer or something or leaves to go out with friends. It's ridiculous."

I decided to test Adam's interest in getting involved in the consultation and asked him if the outcome of the arguments he has with his folks ever seems ridiculous to him as well.

"Sometimes."

"In what way?"

"I don't know. It's all just so stupid sometimes. We fight over the littlest, stupidest stuff."

I didn't push for any more. Any additional compliance and participation from Adam, and he'd start thinking he was being *too* cooperative and have to pull back. Besides, his admission that much of what usually happened was senseless was as close to a peace offering as we were going to get.

I asked Darlene and Evan what they thought accounted for the difference in their family between last year and this. Darlene looked bewildered and shrugged. Evan stated, "There are more rules now. There need to be, because he wants to do a lot of things, and he needs rules for them."

"I don't need rules about going out. I already know how to go out," was Adam's contribution.

Evan explained his perspective. "Adam was always a bit of a hothead, even as a little kid. I think Darlene and I simply got into a bad habit of not pressing issues with him because it would become this whole big thing. It wasn't ever a problem until now, because most of the stuff we would have argued over was small stuff."

"He's never been a bad kid," defended Darlene.

"I'm sure he's not a bad kid now," I said. "But he does seem to have gotten the better of you two over the past few months."

"This is true," Evan said. "Anyway," he continued, "I think

113

we've been having problems now because we're finally putting our foot down about some things. Adam's made some friends this year so he wants to go out. That's fine, but, I mean, he'd stay out until two or three o'clock in the morning if it were up to him. So we make rules and now he fights them."

"Now you each feel as if you have something worth fighting for," I said. "For Adam, staying out with his friends, and for you, making sure he's safe and in at a reasonable hour."

"Yeah," Evan replied, "we sure do feel we have something worth fighting for." He turned toward his son. "Adam, your mom and I just want you, first of all, to be safe, and second, to grow into someone who's happy and able to make good decisions in life and is a pleasure to be around. We're really not trying to bust up your party of being fifteen."

Adam looked at his dad with his first genuine eye contact of the evening.

ADAM's family story is typical of the junctures in the life cycle of families where parents and teens first begin to have explosions between them that cause serious concern. Having managed to navigate the stormy waters surrounding pre- and early adolescent matters—mall trips, clothing, music volume, or telephone or chat room hours—parents and teens occasionally find themselves in over their heads when trying to handle the matters related to middle and late adolescence—dating, curfews, increased exposure to alcohol and drugs, or sexual experimentation. Kids at fourteen or fifteen are more vocal about their opinions than younger kids and will march unhesitatingly into battle to defend their points—even if they are uncertain about what those points are. Combine that with their maturational drive toward independence, and you've got a stage perfectly set for conflict. From the parents' perspective, it's no longer a matter of how long is too long to stay at the mall, but rather into whose car might my son or daughter be tempted to get and how many beers were consumed?

The idea that families go through cycles over the course of their lifetime is one that family and adolescent therapist Jay Haley promoted in the 1970s and 1980s. He described the stages that individuals go through over the course of their lives and the adjustments that must be made in each cycle to avoid problems in the family's stability and functioning. Haley saw many of the problems that client families and individuals were having as being a function not of mental health problems per se, but of difficulties adjusting to changes in their lives as a result of progressing from one stage to another, for instance, changing from being a young married couple to a young married couple with kids, or from a family with young kids to a family with teenagers. Once family members learned to adjust to the changes brought about by a transition from one cycle to another, many of the behavior and emotional problems would recede. What were once considered overwhelming, intractable psychological problems could, through this different lens, now be conceptualized as predictable, even normal, responses to changes in the family as a result of members leaving, coming, entering adolescence, marrying, aging, or dying.

Darlene and Evan were mistaken to think that there had not been a problem in the years before they called for consultation. In truth, all their efforts to avoid conflict and gloss over problems during Adam's younger years set bad precedents for the present. Adam was insisting that the means for keeping peace in the household be kept the same. It had always been that way, and it had worked in his favor. The stakes now, however, were higher, and Darlene and Evan couldn't ignore that without there being dire consequences for them all.

Years ago our family purchased a lovely bullmastiff puppy. Bullmastiffs grow up to be devoted family dogs, affectionate and protective without the aggressiveness of some of the other larger breeds. But they do get big, and they can be stubborn. As we were lunching with our pup's breeder the day we came to pick her up, he said something I never forgot: "She may look irresistable now, but, *from the beginning,* don't let her do anything that you won't want a 125-pound dog doing." That was good advice, and we've followed it. From the beginning, no meant no, down meant down, come meant come. She nearly drowned in our affection for her, but her rules were her rules, and she understood that from the start. Rules helped her recognize her place in the family and set the stage for her to grow into a well-behaved dog that is a pleasure to be around.

That's not bad advice for parents, either: not letting their toddler, preschooler, or grade-school-age kid regularly get away with anything they don't want their teenager doing. If they say no to their three-year-old, she should understand they mean no. They may have to repeat it, explain it, or demonstrate it, but they can't repeatedly "let it slide for now" without creating a problem later. When a little one doesn't oblige, she learns there will be consequences. Those consequences may be a time-out, a talk about being a better listener, or the loss of a special snack. But letting things slide because "three-year-olds can't be expected to behave" (why not, within reason?), or because "I didn't want to cause a fuss" (easier to handle a fuss at three than at fifteen), or because "it wasn't any big deal" (kids learn about the big issues in life by how their parents handle the little things) makes a parent's job harder later.

AT the end of their first session, I told Darlene and Evan that I wanted to meet privately with Adam the following week. In the meantime, I suggested that they spend some time thinking about the different ways in which they had given up control for the sake of (pseudo) peace in their family with regard to Adam's behavior and attitude, and how they could envision assuming it again. I also asked them to consider the following questions:

- What could they anticipate being the most difficult aspects of assuming a more confidently authoritative stance around the household with regard to Adam's behavior?

- What might Adam find hardest and easiest about the changes?

- Where might they expect the most resistance? The least?

- Where could they anticipate getting stuck in the change process? What would persuade them not to make changes now?

- How might each of them inadvertently undermine change?

- How will they recognize any undermining, and what can they do to preempt it?

- How can they best support one another throughout the time of change?

- When will they recognize themselves as a family whose parenting style has changed?

These kinds of questions are oriented toward *finding solutions, promoting real change among family members and the family system,* and *dealing with the present and future.* They stand in sharp contrast to questions that focus a family's attention on their history of problems and their past. I asked Darlene and Evan these questions because I wanted to encourage a proactive parenting stance, so they could anticipate the changes that could take place in the family system and in familial relationships, begin to create a vision of these changes, and prepare themselves for the glitches and bobbles that were inevitably going to accompany a shift in parenting style. My suggestion that they think about these things in the interim between sessions is also a strong communication that the work of the therapy doesn't stop with the end of the session, as well as a vote of confidence in the couple's ability to think for themselves on these matters and contribute significantly to the process.


WHEN Adam returned for his private session, he was as guarded as he had been during the first meeting. Nothing was wrong in his life; his parents hassled him too much; if only everyone would leave him alone there wouldn't be any arguments or problems. He was glib and casual and yawned (fakes, all) repeatedly for my benefit.

I asked Adam what surprised him most about that initial session. At first he seemed taken aback by my question, then bemused.

"I was surprised that it didn't end up being a 'rag on Adam' session. That's what I thought it was going to be about—'Adam never does this. . . . Adam never does that. . . . Adam always needs to have the last word. . . . Adam blah blah blah. . . .' "

"*Do* you always need to have the last word?" I asked, also bemused.

"Sometimes," Adam admitted. "It depends who I'm arguing with." He smiled—the first I'd seen.

This was a significant moment. I would have assumed that Adam needed the last word, but he didn't need to hear that from me. I needed to hear it from him. Letting him tell me something about himself makes the difference between adult/teen encounters that are motored forward by the adult and those that are more collaborative, sustaining the teenager's interest and genuine participation. As soon as the conversation takes on a quality of pulling or leading the teenager along in resigned agreement, the adult has lost any real opportunity to effect changes in the teenager's way of thinking or acting. Adam's acknowledgment that he does, at times, need to have the last word is his way of saying that he will allow me to get to know him as he really is. By not following up his response with questions about why he does that and with advice about learning not to argue that last word is my way of saying to him

that I can be trusted not to pounce on him every time he ad-
mits to some tendency or behavior that irks others. This made
it easier for Adam to settle in and converse with me without
worrying that I was going to try and change him every
chance I got.

I asked Adam, over the course of this meeting, two other
questions that he enjoyed answering. One was, "What is the
one question you think I should have asked at the first session
that would have helped me understand your family better?"
The other was, "What is a question you would have liked me
to ask at that first session that I never did?"

I should have asked, he said, why his parents were willing
to waste their money on therapy when there were so many
other, better things to spend it on, such as new hockey equip-
ment for him and his brother. I ignored this response.

As for a question he would have liked me to ask, it was why
his parents seemed so angry with him all the time and never
wanted to do anything fun with him anymore. I didn't ignore
this one. I asked him what he thought his parents would have
answered had I thought to ask it.

"They probably would have said that it's because I [and
here Adam mimics a parent's complaining voice] 'always cause
trouble whenever we try to do something nice with Adam,
like go out to dinner or to the movies,' " he sneers. "Forget
it," Adam says, changing course. "I wouldn't want to do anything with them, anyway. They're weird, and they embarrass
me to be out with them."

"So do you?"

"Do I what?" Adam asked impatiently.

"Cause trouble?"

"What do you think? You're the shrink here. Don't you know?"

"Of course I don't know. I've never been out to dinner or the movies with you."

Adam gave me a look that said, *You're being more of a wise guy than I am.* "Guess," he challenged.

I gave him a look that said, *Are you sure you want my answer?*

ANY volatile kid worth his or her salt always tries to get the other person to be the first one to go on the defensive, become angry, or otherwise become flustered. Sometimes they do this subtly, sometimes not. Either way, the other party (typically an adult) is left feeling that he or she has lost control over the conversation. It then becomes hard for that adult to justify their point without sounding shrill or punitive, and the situation deteriorates.

Adam tried to get me on the defensive by telling me that I was the shrink and, therefore, should be expected to "know" how he gets even though he knew that I would have no way of knowing. He asked in the hope of discombobulating me. In the past he had probably found that adults took that kind of bait and got wrapped up trying to "clarify" the teenager's misconception (gee, shrinks can be nice people, too) or by trying to avoid the genuine answer for fear of inciting the kid (by circumventing the truth that he would, in fact, presumably be impossible while out at a restaurant). As soon as a teenager discovers that the adult is being "careful" not to get his dander up, he becomes opportunistic. He will keep the adult on the defensive and keep him from believing he can speak freely. Communicating to Adam, even nonverbally, that I believed him to be as difficult as his parents would have said he was told him that he could expect no false peacekeeping from me. Instead, I gave him a candid reflection of my experience with him as a human being.

I didn't see the first flashes of temper Darlene and Evan had described to me until I asked Adam a question he didn't like. Having a tantrum is a loss of control, and the angry kid does not allow losses casually.

Adam had been telling me about all the nice things he does for his younger brother, Seth, including "letting" him use the (family) basketball hoop in the driveway, "allowing" him to sit in the living room when Adam's friends were over to watch a movie, or "giving him the benefit of the doubt" when Adam suspected him of misplacing the TV remote. Adam then described his frustration when Seth had refused to do "one stupid little thing" for him when he does "so many nice things for the kid."

"What was the one stupid thing?" I asked.

"It was nothing—just to patch the one little stupid hole in the wall that I was supposed to fix. It would have taken him a second, and he wouldn't do it."

"Why did you want to pass it off onto him?"

"I was busy."

"Where'd the hole come from?"

"My fist," Adam replied, looking up at me.

This retort was another of Adam's increasingly futile attempts to intimidate.

I remained unastonished. "I don't get it. Why should he have wanted to patch a hole you made?"

" 'Cause I'm his big brother."

"Nah, you're a bully," I corrected him.

"Oh, get out. I don't push anybody around."

I waited, not caring to debate.

"I don't!" Adam insisted. "It's not like I do outrageous stuff like rob cars or sell drugs or set buildings on fire."

"Maybe not buildings, but I heard you made a little cook-out with the kitchen tablecloth instead of washing the dishes."

Adam looked up sharply and cocked his head at me before beginning his defense. "My mom was getting on my nerves," he tried to explain. "She kept asking me and asking me, and I was tired of her nagging. So I got angry! She nags me too much in this stupid little fake sweet voice! She should just yell or something. I was just trying to make a point, anyway. I dumped water on it, and it went right out. It was no big deal. Oh forget it, this is stupid. I'm leaving." Adam got up and marched over to the door.

"Then what? You and your folks are in big trouble with your fighting and fussing and stone silences. Nobody's happy. You know this. Unless you or they have some tricks up your sleeve, it's going to be a long, miserable adolescence for all of you. Why not try something different?"

"Yeah, and what are you going to do to help?"

"I think I can help, and if you'd sit here long enough for me to tell you, I will. For starters, though, I'd say that until you quit feeling like you rule every roost, it's going to be a long haul. Obviously, you like being the big poobah." I smiled. "Be a big poobah if you want, Adam, but just do a better job of it. You'll have more success."

"What do you mean, do a better job of it?" Adam sneered.

"I mean, do it so that people *want* to hear what you have to say instead of waiting for you to finish your tirade."

Adam softens, then quietly asks what a poobah is.

I TOLD Adam what a poobah was that day, and how, if it were his nature to be a poobah, he could be one without needing to butt heads with everyone around him. I made the distinction between leader-like poobahs, whose power people gravitated toward, and the bellowing, boistrous type, whose pseudo-power people resented and dismissed out of hand. I said that I thought I could help him become one of the former. I also told Adam how I viewed the family as one whose earlier efforts to keep the peace was winding up biting them on the behind as Adam reached mid-adolescence. I talked about family life cycles, and how I thought his family was not a bad one but one who had gotten stuck because of their discomfort with being direct and assertive with each other.

I also spoke to Adam of the ways in which I thought he should be more assertive, too, such as instead of letting his mother's "too-careful" manner bug him so much that he sets part of the house on fire, to tell her that he wished she would not walk on eggshells around him. However, I cautioned, he needs to tell her that he won't blow up (which is what she's trying to avert), and actually listen. I took Adam's attention, soft eye contact, and lack of rebuttal as his beginning to endorse this new way for his family to relate. That he didn't make any overt signs of agreement didn't surprise me, and I didn't push for any. Adults sometimes forget that teenagers often make their best changes privately and without fanfare, without ever acknowledging that they have or are considering doing things differently.

DARLENE, Evan, and Adam attended the third session together. I asked Darlene and Evan what the past two weeks had been like for them as a family.

"Better. Some ups and downs," replied Darlene. "I felt that Evan and I were actually more together on a few things regarding Adam, and maybe we handled things more consistently between the two of us. Adam had a few flare-ups when we stayed firm, but nothing too wild."

"It's true," Evan agreed, "Darlene and I worked more as a team—at least I didn't feel as if she was trying to get me to just drop matters with Adam. And Adam had trouble with that, I think."

"I'd have expected some of that," I commented. "Adam liked it the old way. One or two roars, and everyone backed off. He'll probably keep roaring for a little while." I looked over at Adam. I made no mention of our last session's conversation, leaving it to him to decide if and when he'll make the changes we'd alluded to.

"But what do we do if he gets out of control and we can't stop him?" Darlene asked.

"I don't think Adam ever really gets 'out of control.' I think he indulges himself, and your tolerance for his behavioral excesses has actually inflamed blow-ups," I explained. "Expect him to be able to pull his punches, and continue to hold him accountable for his behavior by insisting on retribution. If he ruins dinner with a big hissy fit, send him out to volunteer at a soup kitchen for one whole Saturday. If he says he's not going, refuse to take him anyplace until he does. If he's mean to his brother, he forfeits his Saturday to planning and supervising a pizza and movie party for Seth and his three best friends. Stuff like that."

"Okay, good, I think I got it," laughed Evan. He asked my opinion on how they might have better handled a situation that had occurred just a few days ago. It seems that Adam took it upon himself to invite three friends to sleep over Friday night. Darlene and Evan found out about it when Adam began telling Darlene what he and his buddies wanted for dinner. Darlene told Adam that she and his dad had plans for the evening that didn't include his slumber party. Adam then become irate, claiming that they were going to cause him intolerable embarrassment by not letting his friends stay over. Darlene and Evan held their ground, but Adam showed up with his friends anyway. When Darlene told Adam that he needed to ask his friends to leave by the time she and Evan left for their dinner engagement, Adam exploded. He screamed at his parents that they were selfish and rude to his friends, and he threatened to leave for the night. Adam was still ranting and raving as his friends, far more sensible in this awkward moment than their desperate pal, quietly apologized to Darlene and Evan and slipped out the front door.

"So far so good, guys," I cheered.

"Well, we left Adam at home—still angry—and told him

that he was not to invite anyone over while we were out. Then we went out ourselves."

"What do you mean yourselves? You would have taken Adam?"

"Well," admitted Darlene, "I think in the past we would have tried to smooth things over by maybe inviting Adam out with us to dinner. Not with his friends or anything, but just have him come along."

"After his whole production?" I acted incredulous.

"Uh, yeah."

Adam tried playing to his parents' bleeding hearts. "You should have taken me out with you, you know," he argued. "I can't believe how rude you were being, leaving me home like that."

I let my jaw drop at his pathetic attempt to appear righteous and betrayed but waited for his parents' answer.

"Adam, we weren't trying to be rude, we just need more notice with these kinds of things," appeased Darlene.

I could stay silent no longer. "Hold on, Darlene. Don't start legitimizing Adam's charge of rudeness with an explanation. He knows you guys didn't do anything but respond as any parents should have under those circumstances. Don't let that clever boy play dumb with you! He knows exactly how to properly ask his folks if a bunch of buddies can sleep over."

"That's true," replied Evan. "We should expect more of him and not try to protect him so much from the trouble he gets into."

Adam tried one more time. "Well, all I know is that I can't believe you actually sent my friends away from the house."

"And I can't believe you took such a chance with their

feelings by inviting them over before you knew we were in a position to welcome them," was Darlene's excellent response.

Darlene and Evan and I met again about three weeks later. Adam refused to come, but it didn't really matter. Darlene and Evan were doing well in terms of becoming more comfortable calling Adam on his behavior and asserting their expectations. They more easily tolerated his blustery outbursts and stood firm when he tried to intimidate them with threats of "I'm going to get really angry!" (to which they learned to reply, *So get angry*) or "I'm gonna have to do something!" (which they ignored). Once, when Adam actually did hit the garage wall with his fist, Darlene calmly brought him some spackle and said, "Better get going." When Adam said, "I don't have to do this," she replied, "Then don't." His mother's composed response surprised Adam.

"What if I don't do it?" he asked.

"Then you will simply be making things more difficult for yourself," Darlene replied. "And, by the way, you are paying for the repair supplies out of your allowance. Also, you're grounded for the weekend, and longer if the wall's not done." Later that afternoon, when Darlene, Evan, and Seth were out of the house and no one was watching, Adam fixed the wall.

FOR their final visit one month later, Adam joined his parents. He seemed brighter, lighter, and more relaxed. He initiated some of the conversation and responded thoughtfully to questions. Darlene and Evan reported a remarkably quiet period since the last session and said that not only did they feel they were relating with more candor and frankness toward Adam, but that they felt that he was reciprocating, and in very appropriate ways.

"Do you know that Adam even told me that it always bugged him when I'd try to avoid a problem by staying really calm," said Darlene. "He said he'd rather I just tell him what I really want to. He even said he'd try to listen. How about that. Ha, all these years trying to pussyfoot around my little hothead."

I glanced over at Adam, who was looking a bit sheepish and shy. I winked. It was time to end this session, and the therapy.

According to follow-up telephone contacts with Darlene and Evan, Adam did well over the next few weeks and months. He seemed more willing and better able to express his needs directly, which reduced his explosive outbursts. Darlene and Evan learned to listen to their son more patiently without trying to fix every problem that came up in conversation. Darlene also stopped being so cautious around Adam, something which had so irritated him, and he responded by acting more responsibly about his emotional reactiveness. When Adam would get too hotheaded, Darlene would remind him that if he wanted her not to pussyfoot around the hotter issues, he had to satisfactorily manage his reactions to difficult topics and conversations. He consented. Adam had turned into the decent kid he always could have been, and Darlene and Evan the good parents they aspired to be.

# 8

# MARIAH

## Managing the Secretive Adolescent

*"I'm afraid to look in her backpack because of what I might find—but as her parent I can't afford not to. . . ."*

"They treat me like I'm twelve years old! They won't trust me no matter what, so why should I care what I do anyway?!" Mariah yelled at me as her parents looked on.

"Mariah, we don't treat you like you're twelve. It's just that—"

"You do, too, Ma! I'm so sick of it! You want to know where I'm going, who I'm going there with, what we're doing, when I'm planning to get back, whether I ate anything, whether I burped—it's ridiculous! Forget it! This is a waste."

Mariah's dad turned to me and explains, "Mariah thinks that because she has her driver's license now and has use of a car, she can do as she pleases."

"I *don't* think I can do as I please. I just want to have my own life without the two of you prying all the time. I'm sixteen! I can make my own decisions."

"Yeah," her mom added, "sixteen going on twenty-five."

Mariah shot her mom a look, crossed her arms across her chest, and turned away in her chair.


THE Samuel family's second session was going about as smoothly as the first one. Mark and Sheila brought their daughter in for counseling for a number of reasons, the most critical being her sharply declining school grades and the discovery of a small amount of marijuana in the glove compartment of the family car. Mariah had also become increasingly secretive of late regarding her whereabouts and had adopted an arrogant attitude toward her parents.

Mariah was an only child of professional parents whose work kept them away from home until late in the afternoon or early evening. For the last year Mariah had had the responsibility of caring for herself after school, and for much of that year she'd done pretty well. She had always completed her homework and her chores and started dinner. Mariah entertained herself easily and abided by her parents' rules about not having friends over when her parents were not home. If she had been asked, Mariah would have described herself as a very independent girl. In fact, she so prided herself on her independence that she began to take it too far. She stopped asking her parents for help with homework ("It doesn't count if they help me. It means I'm stupid."). She stopped asking her mom to go shopping with her ("If I can't pick out my own clothes by now, I'm in sorry shape."). She stopped telling them about her friends ("I don't need their help to manage my social life anymore.").

When I had asked Mark and Sheila in that first session when they thought Mariah might have become *too* independent, Sheila blurted, "My Mariah came out of the womb that way! I'll tell you, right from the start she knew what she wanted and what she didn't want. She was some baby."

"And some toddler!" added Mark. "There was no shutting her down when she took a tantrum."

Mariah rolled her head back over at them and stared. She'd obviously heard this innumerable times.

"Mariah has always had a mind of her own. At first it was cute, then it was just difficult to manage. Now it's worrisome," Mark said.

"You don't have to worry, Dad. I'm really fine."

"Then why are you smoking marijuana?"

"First of all, smoking pot has nothing to do with not being fine. Normal kids smoke nowadays, Dad. And second, I don't smoke, so you have nothing to worry about."

"And that bag of marijuana in the glove compartment was just a friend's, right?" pursues Sheila.

"Right, Ma, it was just a friend's," Mariah snaps back.

"Which friend?" asks Mark.

"I'm not saying. That's not your business."

Mark and Sheila looked over at me. *See what we go through?*


CLEARLY, these folks have been butting heads with one another for some time. While no child comes out of the womb looking for a rumble, it is possible that Mariah's native temperament was naturally forceful. Parenting a headstrong child can become a tough ride for parents who are accustomed to older siblings with milder temperaments, or who simply don't have the ability to raise a strong-willed child without exacerbating her innate volatility. These parents might try to counter their child's forcefulness with their own, which results in terrible battles for control between parent and child and possibly the beginnings of a child's difficulty to accept authority comfortably. Alternatively, the parents succumb to the temperamental manipulations of the child and settle for less control in exchange for a tantrum-free household.

It looked to me as if the Samuels had settled on the latter. But Mariah's strong will and independence had also worked in Mark and Sheila's favor. Given their schedule, it was helpful to them to have a child who could take care of herself and who didn't rely too much on her parents. However, the independence that began as a potentially resourceful personality trait wed Mariah to her isolation and inability to accept help, or influence from others.

In our second session, I told them that Mariah always seemed to have prided herself on her independence and that although being independent can certainly be a good thing, it works against you if it keeps you from letting yourself be influenced or touched by others. I shared with them the story of a young woman in her twenties I'd known who longed for some genuine, deep friendships in her life but who found herself unable to cultivate them.

"This woman had spent her adolescent years cultivating an image as someone who had everything under control. She could handle everything. Nothing got to her. *No one* got to her. If she wasn't sure she could achieve it (for example, the respect of a particular teacher, the affections of a certain boy, top-notch grades), she wouldn't allow herself to want it. She lacked for nothing—or so she thought.

"But Jessie grew increasingly isolated and unhappy as she went into and through college. Peers were developing rewarding friendships that eased the adjustment to college life. They gathered in groups and did fun activities together. They seemed happy. She found herself gravitating toward people who had a darker edge, who were cavalier about their studies, who drank too much and had too much casual sex, and whose negativity and sarcasm chased away many of their classmates. Jessie didn't necessarily like these kids, but she felt more comfortable with them than with the others because their darker side matched hers and because she knew they would easily welcome her company. As long as they enjoyed the contact more than she did, Jessie felt in control of the relationships, as meaningless to her as they were."

"So?" asks Mariah. "What's your point?"

"My point is that control and independence alone can add up to a pretty hollow victory."

"So what? I have plenty of good friends."

"I'm sure you do. I have no plans to convince you that your life isn't fine just the way it is. That's for your parents to do. Or your friends, if they feel it's important."

"What are you planning to do then?" Mariah challenges.

"Help your parents insist on parenting you even though you don't think you need them to anymore."

"Oh, like they need more convincing?" Mariah remarks.

I ushered Mark and Sheila out of the office so I could speak with Mariah alone. "Yeah, I think they do," I replied as I returned to my seat. "I think they back down because you put on a good show of being able to handle everything yourself. Then when you get in trouble, they kick themselves for not having stood firm in the first place. So they come down even more strongly the next time. You chafe at their attempts to supervise you and get angry. They back off. And on and on it goes."

"I don't get in trouble."

"Getting caught with stash in the glove box is getting in trouble."

"I don't smoke anymore."

"I have no idea whether you do or whether you don't. The more relevant thing is that neither do your parents. Therefore, they're going to need to check on you more than if they knew you weren't smoking."

"Is that what you're going to tell them?"

"Of course." I shrugged and looked Mariah straight in the eye. "What else *should* I be saying?"

Mariah shook her head softly and sat back in her chair.


Mark and Sheila came without Mariah for the next visit. Before I could sit down, Sheila started to tell me of an incident that had occurred over the preceding weekend.

"Mariah came home, a little late for her curfew. She had two friends with her. I could swear Mariah was high or something. They just acted odd, kind of goofy. Mariah knows she's not supposed to bring friends home at night unless she's asked us beforehand. I don't know, she just was acting strangely, lots of bravado, stuff like that.

"I asked her to please have her friends leave, and she did, with no argument. But she would not let her backpack out of her sight. She hadn't gone upstairs yet so she had it with her, but she wouldn't put it down. At one point I even said, 'Mariah, why don't you put down your pack? It looks so heavy.' She ignored me.

"I let the matter drop, but I wasn't happy. Mark was asleep, and I wasn't sure how far to press the issue."

"Which one?" I asked. "Whether or not she was high, or whether or not she had drugs in her backpack?"

"Both."

"Did you ask her?"

"Not really. Well, I half asked her. I said, 'Are you alright? You seem to be in a strange mood tonight.' "

"How did Mariah respond?"

"By giving me a nothing answer. Something like, 'I'm fine.' "

"Well, if you want a solid answer, you've got to ask a solid question. Although," I added, "with teenagers, even then you're hardly assured of a decent answer."

"What would you have done?" Mark asked.

"I think I would have been very straight with her and told her that she seemed high to me and I was wondering if she had been smoking marijuana."

"I doubt she'd have given me a straight answer," commented Sheila.

"It doesn't matter. You didn't get one anyway. But at least by asking her directly you're telling her that you notice things and that you're not going to pass over your observations just because she may not like what they are."

"What would you have done about the backpack?" Mark inquired.

"I'd have asked her to let me see what was inside it. I'd have explained that I thought she might be high, that I was uncomfortable with and suspicious of the way she was handling her backpack, and that I wished to see its contents."

"I'd have felt so invasive," remarked Sheila.

"Well it is invasive, there's no getting around that. But when a kid who's known to have dabbled with drugs shows up at home acting funny, then all bets are off, and the parents are entitled to check their suspicions. Mariah can't have it both ways. If she wants her privacy respected, she's responsible for walking in her front door in ways that won't make her parents think she's high. If she were doing nothing to suggest she was using, I'd say leave her backpack alone."

This is a point at which many teenagers get their parents feeling as if they're over a barrel. If parents don't press the issue, in this instance checking the backpack for evidence of drug use, they can feel ineffectual or remiss. They worry that being seen as patient, trusting, or nonalarmist compromises their ability to keep their child safe. On the other hand, if they follow their instincts and check, they run the risk of facing the wrath of their adolescent child who feels her trust violated.

"I can't believe you don't trust me!" is a hard-wired adolescent battle call. It needs to be answered honestly. If the parent doesn't trust, he or she must say so.

"Sorry, I don't. I can't. I wish I could."

When parents try to deny their loss of faith in the teenager or apologize for it, they get tangled in a web of defending a position that needs no defense. It seems as if it needs defend-

ing only because *the teenager has defined* the parents' unwilling-
ness to trust them as an outrageous and inexcusable offense to
their growing independence and maturity.

*"I can't believe you don't trust me! That is so rude! How am I
supposed to grow up if you don't even trust me? I can't believe this!"*
the teen screams in an attempt to manipulate a capitulation or
retraction from the parent. The parent who does capitulate
teaches the teenager that trust is something owed to her, in
spite of how it may have been abused in the past. *"Nicole, it's
not that I don't trust you, it's just that I want to make sure . . . ,"*
appeases her father. This is an untruthful statement, and the
kid knows it. The father *doesn't* trust his daughter's words or
judgment, and he should say so, and say why. Doing anything
else robs him of his credibility. It will be very hard now for
this father to help his teenager assume any responsibility for
*why* she isn't trusted with the matter at hand. A better response
would be, *What would you have expected me to say, Nicole? You've
been an hour late coming home for the last three nights you've gone
out. One time you came home, and it was obvious you'd been drinking. You're right. I don't trust your judgment these days, and I don't
trust when you say you'll be home on time. I look forward to when
I'll feel differently, but I need to see you handle things differently
first."*

At times, issues of trust come up between parents and
teenager not as a battle call but as a power play. The teenager
has a secret she knows the parents want to hear about and
taunts her parents with it. The parents can't catch the secret,
however, and the teen taunts more: *I have something you want
to know about, and I am in total control of whether or not you get to
find out what it is.*

This is how Caitlin's mom felt the morning after her daughter had some friends over.

"Honey, what was going on last night among you and all your friends?" Mom inquires. "Everyone looked upset, and I heard Terry's name mentioned and something about how she was in so much trouble with her parents."

"It was nothing," came the reply.

"Nothing? Half of you were crying, and the other half were stomping around down in the basement all angry. It looked like something serious was going on. Can't I help?"

"No, Ma, you can't help. It's nothing." Caitlin turned away and started to leave the room, leaving her mother standing and looking at her.

"Well, I know you're saying it's nothing, but it sure looked like something. You so rarely tell me about your problems, and I feel completely out of the loop with regard to your personal life. Maybe I can't help, but I could lend a supportive ear. And to be honest, I do worry about you and want to be sure you're able to sensibly handle the situations you and your friends get into."

"Look, Ma, I'd like to tell you, but it's just that I can't trust you," Caitlin says.

"Can't trust me? I'm your mother! Of course you can trust me!" Caitlin's mom begins to remind Caitlin of all the times she's demonstrated trustworthiness. And because it has acquired value as a desired commodity, trust becomes a new form of currency to be courted by the parent—or withheld by the teen.

Unlike Caitlin, however, whose secretiveness grew out of a sisterhood's code of silence over something that had happened to a friend, Mariah's evasiveness was designed to keep her parent from knowing about her *own* activities and required more assertive intervening on her parents' part. Her prior breaches of trust also differentiated Mariah's situation from Caitlin's, inasmuch as Caitlin had never tried to deceive her parents about what she did or who she did it with, and added to my reasons for stressing Mark and Sheila's need to more actively intercede when Mariah played the innocent while dragging the crime scene home for everyone to see.

Mark and Sheila left the session that day feeling more confident about their entitlement to know more about what was happening in Mariah's life. They discovered in retrospect that they had "bought into" Mariah's presentation of herself as self-sufficient. As we spoke of her schoolwork, social life, and emotional development, Mark and Sheila were surprised to recognize how diminished their involvement had become over the years and how disenfranchised they were feeling as the agents of supervision and moral guidance in their daughter's life. No wonder Mariah reacted so negatively whenever her parents attempted to intercede in her affairs; she had become accustomed to being able to intimidate them into backing off. Their recent and growing concerns about her moods and attitude, however, made Mark and Sheila feel that they could no longer afford to let that happen.

Before Mark and Sheila left, I explained to them that Mariah was not going to welcome (at least on the surface) any changes they were going to make in their parenting and particularly in their management styles. She'd already spent a few years making many of her own decisions—many of them good ones, in fact—and she wasn't going to appreciate her executive powers being reined in. They could expect, I told them, a fair amount of resistance and loud protests over being "overprotected" and "babied." I told Mariah's parents that such complaints would be understandable and that they should empathize with Mariah but not yield to her demands to go back to the old ways of "hands-off" parenting. Eventually, she'd find that they were not trying to imprison or infantilize her, that the changes were on a much smaller and more subtle scale than she was probably imagining, and that as she demonstrated better judgment over time, her parents could take small steps to back off.

"Talk to Mariah," I encouraged, "and tell her about the kinds of things you'd like to begin doing differently as parents. Explain specifically what you might do or say that will be different, for example, that you want a better sense of whose homes she's going to and whether or not there will be adult supervision. Explain that you'll sometimes want to talk to the parents, or pick her up from friend's houses rather than let her get rides from friends. And finally, tell Mariah that if she chooses to come home and act in a way that makes you suspicious that she's been drinking or smoking pot, that you will investigate."

"What if she wears us down with her protesting?" wonders Sheila, aware of how persistent and overbearing her daughter can be.

"You and Mark should troubleshoot ahead of time for that very thing," I respond. "Consider how Mariah has worn you down in the past, and prepare yourselves for her arguments. Think ahead about how you can respond if she becomes argumentative and how you two can rely on one another, or on

**141**

a friend or relative, for support. Take time-outs if you need to 'consult' with each other if you feel she's getting the upper hand and about to make you change your mind. Bear in mind that the price you pay for *not* avoiding conflict will be small in comparison to the one you would pay if you kept things as they are. Mariah needs you to be more on top of her and she knows it. She'll probably even be relieved at the changes once she stops railing about them. Most kids really do want to know exactly where the lines are drawn."

I met with Mariah a week after her parents went home from this last session. They had called several days later to tell me they wound up talking with her that evening and, after an initial display of outrage and umbrage, Mariah settled into a few days of sulking and acting snippy. She arrived at my office sulky as well; she wasn't happy with the changes I'd encouraged her parents to make with her, and she wanted me to know.

"Tell me about the talk," I asked.

"What talk?" Mariah asked me back.

"You know, the talk that you blame me for."

Mariah smiled in spite of herself and looked down at her sneakers.

"Oh, you mean *that* talk." She tried to act sullen and angry again but had lost her composure. "What's there to tell? Besides, you told them what to say so you already know what the talk was about."

"I know what it was about. I want to know how it *went*."

"It went stupid. My mom and dad are going to put me on house arrest, and I'm going to be bored and miserable for the next three years until I can finally get out of there and have a life."

"Then that was some other therapist's doing, not mine." I tried to catch Mariah's eye with my smile, but she wouldn't let me.

"Well, it just is going to feel like that, anyway."

"I suppose it might for a while. You really ran your own show there for a long time. You had your very own kingdom, and now the king and queen want the thrones back."

"Well, they never should have given them up in the first place if they were going to change their minds."

"They probably shouldn't have ever given them up, but not because they'd want to change their minds later. They shouldn't have given them up because they needed to be the ones in charge. But maybe they didn't realize how important that was for a kid, or maybe they thought they *were* in charge.

"But I'll tell you something else, too, Mariah. You're a pretty independent girl and seem to have always enjoyed making your own decisions. I suspect that somewhere along the line you managed to convince your folks—whether you ever meant to or not—that, for the most part, you were capable of managing your affairs. So they figured, 'Okay, Mariah's doing all right, we don't need to worry about her.' And busy as they were, it worked for them, too. You oversold your abilities, and they too easily allowed themselves to be convinced."

"So now what?" Mariah asked softly, head down.

"So now you guys have to spend some time figuring out how it's going to work between two parents who aren't comfortable enforcing limits that make you mad at them, and one kid who'd like to think she's pretty much grown up and doesn't need all that meddling but maybe, privately, welcomes their involvement in her life."

Mariah sat quietly for a long time before leaning back in the chair and sighing deeply.

THE final session I had with the Samuels included Mariah, Mark, and Sheila. It took place about three weeks after my session with Mariah and revealed a family clearly in the process of redefining itself. Mark and Sheila had effectively embraced their broadened responsibilities as parents of an adolescent with some kinks in her judgments and attitudes, but were simultaneously sympathetic to the conditions of diminished autonomy Mariah was now experiencing in her life. Mariah had made her fuss for a while but eventually realized that her parents weren't laying down anything resembling the martial law she'd imagined. She fought them because, as a self-respecting adolescent, she thought she had to. Once she learned that they were less disturbed by her tantrums and had learned how to team up together rather than allow Mariah's argumentativeness to get *them* arguing, Mariah stopped being quite so bullish about things. Her grades picked up, and there were no further indications of pot smoking. On one occasion Mark did challenge Mariah when he came upon her hiding something in her backpack. She argued about privacy rights, but Mark stood firm and said that he wasn't yet comfortable taking her at her word and wanted to know what it was she was hiding. It turned out to be a condom. Bursting into tears and swearing she'd never had sex and was afraid to, Mariah sat down with her dad and confided in him about problems she'd been having with her boyfriend (who Mark and Sheila hadn't even known about), who was pressuring her to become sexually active. They talked for an hour that night about boys and relationships, about sex and pressure, about dignity and self-esteem, and about saying no. Mark was stunned to realize that it was their first talk about this kind of stuff. He'd always considered it Sheila's province, but now he recognized a daughter's need to hear from her father the same things she hears from her mother. The secrets and unspoken issues in this family were finally dissolving.

# 9

## DAVID

### Helping the Depressed, Irritable Adolescent

*"He's just so miserable that I hate to ask him
to do anything. . . ."*

"If I could take whatever it is he is dealing with and bear it myself, I would in a minute," stated David's father, Douglas. "It kills me to see him so unhappy, although he tells me he's not unhappy. He says he's just annoyed at everything all the time and wishes that everyone, including or especially his mom and I, would leave him alone. Annoyed, unhappy—what's the difference? He still seems plain miserable. And we don't know what to do."

David is a seventeen-year-old who has long-standing depression, school problems, and an unwilling attitude around the house. Hannah, David's mom, is with Douglas for this first visit to my office, but David is not. He refused to come, so I told Douglas and Hannah to come on their own.

Douglas and Hannah told me how they and their two

daughters have lived in the shadows of David's moodiness and argumentativeness for years. His depression was the kind that manifested as irritability rather than sadness, although David probably spent long periods of time feeling sad. When he felt good, David was the funniest guy around, they said. Witty and ineffably charming, he would have his sisters and parents roaring with laughter. He was also very generous, especially to his sisters. When he felt good, he offered rides to friends' homes or cooked them his homemade spaghetti dinners. Most of the time, however, David was not funny or generous. He was picky, selfish, and self-absorbed. His family loved him dearly, but they found him hard to live with.

David had a long history of doing poorly in school. He suffered from learning disabilities that made it hard for him to process oral information from his teachers and to synthesize different kinds of information into a coherent body of knowledge. He did not enjoy learning or being in school. He argued with his teachers and, in the earlier grades, found it gratifying to be sent down to the principal's office. He loved to ruffle the feathers of those who valued self-composure. He especially loved an audience.

What frustrated everyone was that David was very smart. He had an excellent memory, grasped abstract concepts well, and intuitively understood social relationships. He read avidly and learned easily outside of the classroom. He did not, however, do well when told what to do.

David's mother had learned to accommodate his personality quirks over the years. When he was in one of his moods, she brought up only "easy" topics, made few demands, and largely left him alone. She picked up his slack around the house, made excuses for why he wasn't coming down for dinner, and even did his chores. Hannah bought off her son's contentiousness with her obliging, conflict-avoidant nature. David, in return, appeased her with pseudo-compliance, small talk, and gratuitous displays of superficial affection. They both knew but never openly acknowledged that if there were something David felt strongly about doing or not doing, his wishes would prevail.

David's father, on the other hand, did not so easily accommodate his son's behavior and poor attitude. He understood that David did not like being told what to do, but that didn't stop him from telling him what he thought he *should* be doing, and when, and how. When David would demur further, Douglas would press the issue, raise his voice, and impose consequences. He was often very angry with his son, and his son with him. They spent long stretches of time not getting along.

For the second session, I asked Hannah and Douglas to bring in all three kids. Shelby (fifteen), Jackie (fourteen), and David waltzed into my office, masking their anxiety by pretending to joke with one another. They proceeded to spread themselves out on the one couch in the room, feigning boredom. Hannah and Douglas entered the room behind them and sat in single chairs on either side of the couch. David, the obvious ringleader of the younger set, decided to play. He looked around at the members of his family and, careful to avoid eye contact with me, cheerfully and facetiously asked them how he could be of service in their time of trouble.

The girls cracked up, but David's parents did not. They looked at him sternly. David waved his eyebrows at his sisters and displayed mock contrition. He'd made his strike and would now be content to remain in the background.

Not wanting to play to David's attempts at humor, nor rescue the family from the discomfort of their anxiety, I waited for them to find another way to begin. It would have been easy for me to have said something to put them at relative ease, but David would have construed my help as placation and an expression of discomfort with tension. In order for the therapy to work, he needed to understand that I would never be more uncomfortable with his anxiety and the anxiety he evoked within the family than he would be. It would have to matter to him more than to me that he got help.

Douglas spoke next. "This is a perfect example of what happens in this family, Janet. We try and get together to address something serious, and one of the kids makes a joke of it. Usually it's David. The other kids follow suit, and then the whole thing goes down the tubes."

"Why do you think it's so difficult for David to be serious about something important?" The question was said for David's benefit, directed toward Douglas, but unmistakably open to anyone.

The two sisters looked at each other and then at David for direction. He had turned pensive and offered them nothing. I gazed over their way and silently asked again with a shrug of my shoulders and hands.

"I don't know," responded Shelby, the older of the two girls. "None of us is really ever serious," she added, in her brother's defense. She looked over to him for approval, but he ignored her.

"If it were up to my parents, we'd be serious all the time," said Jackie, trying to keep up with her sister. "They hate when we joke around."

"Jackie," countered Hannah, "come on, that's not true. Dad and I love to see you guys having fun, but it's just that we can't ever seem to get you to take anything seriously. Like this appointment, for instance."

"Well, I don't understand what this appointment is for anyway, so I can't take it seriously," Jackie declared.

"It's for David, Jackie," said Shelby, putting on a show of annoyance at her sister's insipidness.

That was enough for David. "This appointment isn't for me. It's for you guys to learn how to better deal with me. I'm dealing with me just fine." The alienation of his sisters was now complete. Shelby and Jackie, having found themselves unable to align with their brother and sustain his favor, retreated glumly into silence. David, though, had inadvertently moved front and center into the session but was without the shield of his sisters.

"What is it your parents and sisters have to learn in order to better deal with you?" I asked David.

"They need to learn to be more easygoing, I think. Not worry so much about me, get off my case about stuff. That's all. Then we'll be fine."

Hannah and Douglas had been right about their children's—especially David's—inability to address serious matters directly. What they hadn't mentioned yet was how cavalier their son could get.

"Is David always this flip?" I asked David's parents.

David looked over at me for an instant and then looked over at his parents.

"Yes," replied Douglas, "David is always this flip, and it drives me crazy. He tries to be so clever, and sometimes he is, but other times it's off-putting because we really can't talk to him about stuff that matters." Douglas turned to face his son. "And I would really like to be able to talk to you about stuff that matters sometimes."

"What is mattering now?" I asked.

"David seems unhappy. We all think it, and Hannah and I discuss it, but David will have no part of that conversation. If we bring it up, he shuts us down. Then he acts all righteous, as if we've insulted him by even suggesting that all is not right with him and his world."

Silence fell, as if to affirm Douglas's observations. "I just wish he'd let us help him through this."

"I don't need help 'getting through this,' " sneered David.

"David," came Hannah's plaintive response.

"Mom, don't. Don't 'David' me. I hate that. You guys have been sitting here and talking about me as if I can't speak for myself. Well, I can." And then he stopped.

"Well go ahead then," snapped Shelby. "You're always saying what you're going to do, but you never do it." David cocked his head and glared at his sister. She was going to make him pay for his earlier betrayal.

"You don't know what you're talking about," came David's reply.

"Whatever," said Shelby.

"Shelby, what doesn't David follow through with?" I asked. I was not directly addressing David yet because he was not ready to talk to me. He was beginning to take the session more seriously now, but he was still fighting both it and his parents' concerns. I was still a stranger. Questioning him at this juncture would only have provided David with an opportunity to shut the session down by responding negatively to me.

"I don't know. Ask him." Shelby saw a chance to shift loyalties back toward her brother, and she took it. She had strayed too far for her own comfort.

"I would love to ask David," I responded, while glancing over at her brother, "but I worry he'll shut me down like he does all of you when you tell him you're worried about him or are unhappy with something he does."

"Oh, now are you worried about me, too?" David asked. This was a legitimate invitation, and I accepted.

"Of course I am. Somewhat from what I hear; mainly from what I see."

"Oh, and what do you see?" David's sarcasm belied his curiosity.

"I don't know, I see you shadowboxing like there's no tomorrow. You blow off your parents who are worried that you're unhappy, and you do the same to your sisters when you have no immediate use for them."

"What do you mean, no immediate use?"

"If they aren't going to laugh for you—or cheer for you. They love you and obviously think the world of you, but I think they feel used."

"Used?" David turned toward his sisters and asked, mockingly, *"Do you feel used?"*

Jackie and Shelby tried to grin but were having trouble. Instead, their faces looked strained.

"They can't tell you, David. They want to, but they're too

afraid of losing your approval. They're worried you'll punish them if they say the wrong thing."

*"Punish them?"* David's continued responses told me that he remained interested in what I was saying despite his scorn.

"Sure, punish them by withdrawing your attentions, by giving them the cold shoulder. That kind of stuff."

David rolled his eyes and looked over at his sisters, trying once again to get a laugh. They tried their best to oblige but mustered little more than a fleeting smile.

The room fell silent for a while. David looked lost and fidgeted with the cuff of his jeans. The session ended shortly afterward, but not before Douglas had said out loud, and to no one in particular, "I've never seen David let something go without getting in the last word."

THE third session took place a week later. David was not there. He had managed to set up a summer job interview at exactly the same time as the therapy appointment. I left Shelby and Jackie in the waiting room and met with Hannah and Douglas alone. I'd have lost David forever if he felt that his sisters were involved in a "treatment team" for him in his absence.

I asked Hannah and Douglas what happened after they left the prior session.

"David moped about for a couple of days, but I did notice him treating his sisters differently," said Douglas. "Not anything obvious or even explainable. He just seemed to be a little more *aware* of them around the house. Usually he just ignores them unless he has something he wants to say to them or do with them. I don't know, maybe they were different with him—less obliging or something."

Hannah added more. "I noticed something, too, although it's hard to put it in words. It's almost like he wants to handle things differently so he can't be called on it anymore. But he wants to do it in a way that no one takes notice of."

"Hannah's right. It is like that. He's a funny boy."

"He may be a funny boy, but he's a genuine teenager," I said. "Kids like David—proud, smart, sly, a little arrogant—find it hard to be called on stuff they know to be true. They won't deny it outright, but they silently vow to eradicate the problem just so they don't have to suffer again what they feel is the humiliation of someone telling them something negative about themselves. They may slip back to old habits from time to time, but they will make a concerted—albeit very private—effort to change, not because they believe they should, but because they can't stand being wrong."

"But you never told him he was wrong for treating his sisters the way he does," remarked Hannah.

"I know. And I never told him to do anything about it. I just told him what I was observing. Sometimes it's easier for adolescents to change when it's not something they've been told to do." I added, "That's true for some adults, too."

The rest of the session was spent discussing what it was that Hannah and Douglas wanted to see different in David. How would they know things were improving for their son and family? What would be signs that David either was feeling less depressed and irritable or at least handling his moodiness in a more constructive manner? Furthermore, how might they come up with ways to help David take better advantage of traditional learning environments? And what would be appropriate consequences for David's reluctance to help around the house? How might he try to undermine those consequences with his wit and humor?

Hannah and Douglas agreed to sit down with David privately and express their concerns to him about his chronic unhappiness, while at the same time letting him know that they were no longer willing to be unhappy with him. They were going to tell him that they would do everything in their power to work through the reasons for his discontent with him but not allow his mood to dictate the mood of the household. They would expect him to do chores around the house, and there would be consequences if he didn't. He would be held accountable for his choices.

"What kind of consequence is appropriate for a seventeen-year-old who doesn't bring down his laundry?" asked Douglas.

"The natural one of having no clean clothes," I responded, then paused. "Don't tell me you've been doing his laundry for him under those circumstances. . . ." Douglas looked over at Hannah, who looked away sheepishly.

"Hannah?" I asked.

"Well, I have been guilty of that, I have to admit. It's just that I worry he's going to, you know, look ridiculously sloppy or even *smell* or something! I worry what his friends are thinking. It's not like he has enough friends to spare. So I gather the stuff up and stick it in the machine. I guess you think I shouldn't be doing that?" Hannah looked up at me.

"Well, here's what I think. As long as good hygiene remains more important to you than to your son, you will forever be making sure he washes behind his ears."

"But I'm worried he'll just let it go, skip showers, wear whatever isn't stuck to the floor."

"He might."

"Well, then what?" asked Hannah.

"Then, whatever. If he's bad enough his friends will tell him to go bathe. Believe me, it's not as gratifying when it's your friends instead of your mom."

"Okay. I can do that. But what about how depressed or angry he seems? Can't we do something to help him with how he's feeling?"

"Yes. But David has to give us some window of opportunity, and so far, he's keeping everyone at bay. Trying to help a kid who is working hard to pass himself off as someone not in need of help will wind up feeling like an imposition to him and probably incur its fair share of resistance. I've found the best way to facilitate a conversation about what one is feeling or thinking is to hold that person accountable for what he or she does and says. When they bump up against a boundary that says, *We believe this to be your responsibility, even if you don't,* they wind up speaking out about all kinds of things. Then you'll be able to glean what it is that's truly troubling them."

The session ended after a discussion of how Hannah and Douglas could learn to balance their concern and compassion for David with their apparent need to set firmer limits with him. Parents of children who are unhappy are at risk to become too soft with their discipline; understandably, it's hard for them to come down on their child when they feel they will just be adding to their child's misery. This reaction actually compounds the problem. The child begins to feel as if less is expected of him because he is capable of less, and he becomes more unhappy. Alternatively, the child learns that he can easily put one over on others and becomes frightened of this ability.

Hannah and Douglas understood that they did David no favors by not addressing his dismissive attitudes and recalcitrance. They realized that the sources of his discontent and misery would never be revealed as long as he could continue to both manage and mask his inner life with his offending actions. They committed to changing the way they handled things around the house, especially as it concerned David, and to let more of the responsibility for his personal matters fall squarely on his shoulders.

The next session took place two weeks later, and everyone in the family attended. David appeared a little more lighthearted. He joked with his sisters in the beginning, but it seemed more genuine and less divisive in terms of the two generations of people in the room.

"How long do we have to keep coming here?" asked Jackie. Hannah looked over at her daughter and was about to hush her when I answered her question.

"That's up to your folks to decide, but I imagine that when things work more smoothly at home—and when David no longer tries to rule the household with his moodiness—you'll be spending your Thursday evenings elsewhere."

"Things work fine at home. There's nothing to smooth over," replied Shelby. She had resumed the role of David's defender.

"Things have worked tolerably at home, Shelby, because everyone has always been very careful not to upset David. But it's not a good way for a family to live."

"Careful *not* to upset me? Are you kidding? You guys *love* to upset me," retorted David. "It's your version of family game night."

Douglas joined in. "What David thinks of as us loving to upset him are our attempts to set some limits. And as you already know, there haven't been all that many to begin with. We really haven't asked too much. I don't think we've been asking enough."

"You *haven't* been asking enough," said Jackie. Everybody turned toward her, surprised.

"Give it up, Jackie. You cause your fair share of problems around the house, too, you know," said David, testily.

"Yeah, but not like you."

"That's because you're not as clever. My problems are smart problems because they bother you and don't bother me. Your problems are stupid problems because they bug you and I could give a crap."

David was a boy on a mission to maintain such an edge about himself that no one would dare venture in close. He was barbed wire incarnate, a lonely prisoner of his own warring wit. He hadn't a clue how dearly it was costing him.

But David began to find out. His parents scheduled more sessions and brought the kids. Little by little, through tense and awkward conversation, all five family members discovered how routinized—and limiting—their styles of relating to one another were. Shelby resented Jackie's candor and relative independence of David and so reacted to her forthrightness with anger. Jackie had been feeling that Shelby sold herself out to please her brother and was too willing to accommodate David's demands for loyalty without requiring enough in return. In the process, Jackie had lost respect for her sister. Hannah had already begun to see how her efforts to protect David from his weaknesses had been serving only to entrench him further in an identity as a "no-can-doer," much to his disadvantage. And Douglas was learning how to demand more from his son without becoming overbearing.

David was learning some things, too. He was learning that letting people be on his side didn't make him a weaker human being. He was learning that being in a bad mood was no protection from being expected to uphold his responsibilities. He was learning that making people laugh was less important than being able to make people smile. And finally, he was learning that he wasn't the only person in his family who could have a good idea.

David made some significant changes in his demeanor over the course of the next couple of months. He became softer in his interactions, less sarcastic, and more patient. He listened more. He spent more time downstairs with the family. He often did chores without having to be hounded into it. He occasionally made a spaghetti dinner for everyone.

Jackie, likely in response to the changes in David, began to challenge him less. She stopped leaving the room when he came in. She started borrowing his T-shirts again. Shelby got along with David as she always had, but she was getting along better with Jackie, who seemed now to be less resentful of her sister's devotion to her brother. Hannah had learned how not to accommodate David's self-indulgences and, as a consequence, began having more direct conflict with him. She found she minded this less than she had expected to. "It's not so bad, really. I get to say more of what's on my mind and don't feel as if I have to be so *careful* around him all the time. I used to think I was so bad at standing my ground. I was kind of embarrassed to do it, but you know, it's not so bad. *I'm* not so bad at it!"

Because Hannah had changed her relationship with David, David could change his relationship with his dad. No longer the sole enforcer of rules and regulations, Douglas was freer to show David some of his other, softer sides. David dropped his belligerence, and for the first time in ages, accepted his father's invitations to lunch, a conversation, or an occasional movie.

David didn't fare as well at school as he did at home in the wake of these changes. It appeared he'd been sour on classrooms for so long, and had such adversarial relations with so many teachers and administrative and guidance personnel over the past two years, that when he returned in September for his senior year, he found he couldn't get himself engaged in anything about the school or his classmates. After discussing it among David, his parents, and myself, and after consultation with an educational placement specialist, David and his parents decided to try a private school. It would mean they'd need to borrow from family to cover the tuition, but because it would be for the one year, they felt it was both manageable and worthwhile.

David did well with a fresh start in a school that taught kids with learning problems. Many of the strategies were the same as those the public school had tried to put in place but were rejected by David's earlier need to be seen as too psychologically complex a person to be helped by anything as mundane as a change in educational approaches. In addition, the new school was known for its eccentric, artsy, and edgy student body, something David easily embraced. No longer depressed, righteous, and isolated, he could put his native intelligence to better use than being cunning and contemptuous. Within the first quarter of school, David became a peer leader and, to nobody's great surprise, a fabulous debater. Few who went up against him ever won, but they were always treated in the end to a solid handshake and a gracious smile from a politician in the making.

# *Conclusion*

■

## 10

---

# NOTHING YOU SAY WILL MATTER UNTIL *YOU* MATTER

There are few experiences as lonely or as frustrating as feeling unable to influence someone you care deeply about. It can also be frightening. Mothers and fathers of children who have learned to use emotional reactivity to disarm their parents are rightfully concerned about how they can regenerate and sustain an active, useful, and respectable role in their adolescent's life.

A parent's loss of credibility and the subsequent loss of the ability to influence and affect the child starts early and invisibly in the parent-child relationship. Simple incidents involving a need to share, speak up, help out, apologize, show concern, or respect privacy abound in daily life, and all offer options for response. Some responses favor the fatigue of the overwhelmed, exasperated parent, who doesn't have the time or patience in that moment to address the issue in more than an immediate and perfunctory way: *Forget it, I'll do it. You take forever, and we've got to go.* Others favor the common parental misconception that young kids can't appreciate anything but the most basic things about life and relationships. However, children of three and four years of age are ripe for learning about the concepts of accountability, justice, charity, and self-restraint. These are the basics and are the foundation for family and community living.

Little of significance happens between two people unless at least one matters to the other. The connection can be symbolic, as reflected in prejudice or nationalism, or it can be real, between people who know each other. But nothing anyone ever says to another person will have any influence unless the speaker matters to the person being spoken to. This is felt poignantly by a parent who knows that nothing she will say will stop their daughter or son from leaving the house without permission, getting high that night, or flunking out of school. It is a terrible and helpless experience. A parent can matter and still not get the response she wants; sometimes there are overriding internal or peer pressures for the adolescent, healthy or not. But a parent can never *not* matter and expect to get that teenager's full attention.

How can parents matter strongly enough to their growing children that their sphere of influence remains intact in spite of the encroachment by adolescence?

## Start Early

Four-year-old Sam tries to take a toy away from his ten-year-old sister, Olivia. She discovered it first from among the many toys in my office toy bin and is in the process of enjoying it immensely. She is behaving like a princess of patience in the face of her brother's unrelenting demands.

"Olivia, he's only four years old. Can't you just let him have it?!" exclaims the girl's mother.

No, Olivia can't. And she shouldn't be expected to. In that moment, this little girl understood more about fairness than her mother. To make her give the toy to her screeching brother teaches her that you stand to gain more by exasperating the grown-ups than by playing by the rules. Olivia had found that toy by herself, had not wrested it from anyone's hands, and had neither teased nor taunted her covetous brother. She could have been told she'd eventually need to share her treasure after she'd had it a little while. Instead, she was told to give it up.

"Well fine, if you two can't get along, neither of you gets the toy!" shouts the mother.

Sam amplifies his tantrum, mother appeases him with baby talk, and Olivia storms off, incensed. No wonder she grows up resenting her "baby" brother. No wonder she begins questioning her mother's sense of justice.

To have helped Sam understand that his behavior served only to delay his access to the toy he wanted would have been a gift. Instead, his mother tried to make him feel better, be less angry, and act less disruptively. Sam *was* capable, in that instance, of refraining from screaming and grabbing. His mother's response, however, taught him that he was not, or that even if he was, he was not expected to contain his temper. By virtue of his tender age, he'd been given the bye of overindulgence.

Sam lost the opportunity to learn about appreciating, or at least respecting, another's good fortune—that of Olivia's virgin find. Kids Sam's age understand plenty about relationships, even if some of their understanding is rudimentary. Sometimes they understand more than they are capable of effecting, but that's okay, too. Over time, and with repeated exposure, a child's conception of what it means to be part of a community, be it of two or two thousand, crystallizes. It becomes the operative force behind her actions and words and shapes all subsequent social intercourses.

To learn these lessons kids don't need to feel as if they're enrolled in a lifelong course on modern ethics, or feel badly about themselves, or resent their parents. These lessons are taught through patient explanation, fable, or example. They are the kind that make kids feel valued and valuable; that braid generosity and empathy into the fabric of their characters; and that yield perspective, flexibility, tolerance, and self-respect. They draw children toward, not away from, the parent who is seen as a semi-heroic figure, teaching and modeling and living very simple but heroic kinds of ideals.

## Use Your Self

Rachel and her dad don't talk much anymore, and neither of them knows what to do about it. Rachel has just had her sixteenth birthday and isn't even sure she wants to do anything about it. They've taken to making little digs at each other, but the digs stopped being funny months ago. The teasing has turned sarcastic; the silence, awkward. Rachel's dad wonders if this is normal for adolescent girls and their dads or if it is a sign of something amiss. He wants desperately to change their relationship, but he does not know how to begin.

"I try asking her about her school, her friends—anything to get her to talk to me," her dad tells me. He is sad and seems heartbroken. "I don't know what else to try. If I ask her to go to the movies with me, she says we won't want to see the same film. If I tell her I'll see whatever she wants to see, she tells me to stop trying so hard to be the perfect dad. I'm not trying to be perfect; I'm just trying to stay in her life."

"Tell her that," I advise the father. "Tell her that you could care less about being perfect but want more than anything not to lose your connection to her. Let her know that you know relationships between parents and their teenage children change over time, but that you still want something, and that she still needs something. Tell her you miss talking together. Tell her you miss *her*."

Candor and vulnerability are two of a parent's most powerful vehicles for staying connected to their kids as they move through adolescence and toward independence. They bridge gaps that yelling, crying, demanding, and imploring could never begin to close. Sometimes it pays to get softer when the going gets harder.

## Never Undermine

Parents who feel at their wits' end with their defiant or disengaged adolescent son or daughter can find themselves doing or saying things they never would feel proud of doing. In the spirit of provoking a different response from their teen, they do things that demean and say things that hurt.

Many fractures in the relationship between parent and child may go unaddressed, but they are never undetected. Children grow up with profound resentment for the parent who tries to egg them on through humiliation and sarcasm. They turn off, turn away, go off, or go away. Emotionally, they may not come back. No one has ever been inspired to become a better person through degradation.

Other fractures are more subtle. A parent gets defensive (*"She's impossible to talk to. . . ."*), self-protective (*"I need to see him make the first move. . . ."*), and retaliatory (*"Since she was so nasty about saying I should 'get out' more, I am going to do exactly that tonight and take the car she was planning to use. . . ."*). Tell the daughter that her nasty comment is inappropriate and revoke car privileges for the night if it was that bad, but don't swipe the car out from beneath her under the guise of "doing only what she said you should do." Being mad is never a good reason to pull rank and act unjustly. Parents get a lot more by being firm but temperate.

Taking the high road in these instances also requires that parents help their teenagers find a dignified path out of the dilemmas they have created for themselves. Appreciating and sometimes vocalizing their quandary—their need to save face while simultaneously exiting the corner they've painted themselves into—can break the inertia of unresolved tensions and move the teenager forward. Such an exit strategy might consist of no more than a quiet agreement that the parent not chide the teen for her earlier sense of righteousness about what turned out, as predicted by the parent, to have been a poor choice or ill-considered handling of a matter. What must remain paramount in the parent-teen relationship for the successful navigation of adolescence and early adulthood is the parent's palpable and ever-present respect for the *person* of the teenager, regardless of how angry, hurt, or frustrated that parent is feeling in the moment.

## Staying Connected Must Always Be Seen as Being More Important Than Being Right

Being right should never be more important than the relationship between two people who really matter to each other. Unfortunately, the need to be right and make points ceaselessly become wedges between loved ones.

"That boyfriend of yours was trouble from the word *go*."

"No, he wasn't, Mom. He just changed over the summer."

"Changed, shmanged. Believe me, he was always that way. You just didn't see it. You never do until it's too late."

"You were in a terrible mood last night and took it out on all of us."

"No, I wasn't, Dad. I was in a little bit of a bad mood because of school, but I was trying not to take anything out on anyone. Maybe I was kind of grumpy, but I actually thought you were also a little grumpy yourself. Maybe it was just a bad day for everyone."

"I don't think so, Jessica. I can tell when you are in a bad mood, and you were definitely in one last night."

"Ma, I swear my boss cut my hours because he's cutting everyone's hours. Business is slow."

"He cut your hours because you probably do there what you do here—move too slow and too late. You'll never hold down a job until you develop better work habits."

"I'm actually pretty good at my job, Ma. You should see."

"I should see you be pretty good at your jobs around here first! Then I'll come see."

Sometimes the wedge is insidious and disguised by philanthropy.

Nick long ago lost interest in going camping with his dad. "There was always a right way to do something and a wrong way to do something, and it got so the whole camping trip became this big lesson about how to camp correctly," Nick explained. "The *correct* way to pitch a tent, the *correct* way to start a fire, the *correct* way to roast a marshmallow, the *correct* way to pee in the woods. All I wanted to do was hang out with my dad, but he couldn't stop *teaching* me. It's as if he didn't know how to talk to me without instructing me. I stopped wanting to go."

Relationships with children are sacred, but being sanctimonious doesn't work. Being seen as right, being heard, and getting one's point across have only relative importance compared to the value of preserving those relationships. Where the situations are more urgent, the parent can afford to speak more urgently. A teenager who is using drugs, having premature or irresponsible sex, driving recklessly, or involving himself in other dangerous activities needs a parent who will step in and enforce limits that reflect what that parent thinks is right. But to expect that the adolescent will immediately sign off on the restrictions and recognize them as in his best interests is to expect too much—not because the kid can't see that their institution has merit, but because to him, saying so means that he is telling everybody that he messed up. It's a lot easier for a rebellious, indignant teenager to admit to himself that his parent is right if the admission is not yoked to his having to make external acknowledgments that he was wrong. Sometimes a parent has to let the teenager save face by absolving him of the need to prove his good faith.

People joke about teenagers being difficult company—especially if they live in one's home. "Got any kids? Want mine?" is an old and familiar refrain.

But teenagers aren't that impossible, and most parents aren't, either. None of us, really, is a stroll through the park. We are all creatures of habit and strong beliefs and often think we know better. Whether we do or don't, however, isn't as important as what we have going between ourselves and the people about whom we care deeply. Children come to us largely unshaped, and the responsibility for their upbringing is monumental. It is wonderful when it's done well. How heartening it is when you see it taking place in your own home.

# INDEX

Accountability for behavior
  credibility loss of parents and, 54
  depressed adolescent (David) family story,
    146–61
  parental authority, neutralized, 9–10, 20–21
  volatile adolescent (Adam) family story,
    125–28
Acknowledging behavior changes, 100–101
Adam family story. *See* Volatile adolescent
  (Adam) family story
*Adolescence: The Farewell to Childhood* (Kaplan), 34
Adolescent rights, 92–96
Affection, demonstrating, 11
Anticulturalism, 33–34
Approval of teenagers, soliciting, 55–57
Assertive intervening from parents, 134–35,
  139–42, 144
Assertiveness of teenagers, 124, 128
Authority of parents. *See* Parental authority

Bailing teenagers out, 84–86
Behavior
  acknowledging behavior changes, 100–101
  changing, space for, 98–102
  *See also* Accountability for behavior; Ex-
    cuses for behavior
Blamelessness, perception of, 5

Candor
  for connection to children, 166–67
  for responsibility discussions, 88–89
  for saving face, 101–2
Can't vs. won't teenagers, 69–71
Careful, being too
  credibility loss of parents from, 57–59
  personality styles and parenting, 39–40
Changing behavior, space for, 98–102
Choosing battles, 53–54
Collaborative discussions
  overindulged teenagers, 31

volatile adolescent (Adam) family story,
  119–20
Compensating for something else style, 48–51
Confidence for parenting, 11
Conflict avoidance
  parental authority, neutralized, 3–4, 6–7, 11,
    12
  secretive adolescent (Mariah) family story,
    141–42
  volatile adolescent (Adam) family story,
    115–16, 117
Conflict-avoidant personality style, 38–43
Connection to children, 163–71
  candor for, 166–67
  importance of connection, 163–64
  overindulgence, 165
  relationships, understanding, 165–66
  right, being vs., 169–71
  saving face, need for, 168–69, 171
  starting early, 164–66
  undermining children, 167–68
Consequences of decisions, parental control of,
  68–69, 82–84
Coordinated front, presenting, 48
Creativity vs. leniency, 63
Credibility loss of parents, 52–66
  accountability vs. excuses for behavior, 54
  approval of teenagers, soliciting, 55–57
  careful, being too, 39–40, 57–59
  choosing battles, 53–54
  creativity vs. leniency, 63
  disrespect of teenagers, 52–53
  excuses, making for teenagers, 25–29,
    65–66, 146–47
  excuses vs. accountability for behavior, 54
  expectations, lowering for teenagers, 65–66
  gratuitous compliments vs. self-esteem
    building, 64
  impulsiveness of teenagers, 54
  leniency vs. creativity, 63

174

# Index

# ABOUT THE AUTHOR

**Janet Sasson Edgette, Psy.D., M.P.H.,** has been a clinical psychologist for fifteen years, providing services to children, adolescents, adults, couples, and families. She speaks nationally to mental health professionals on adolescent therapy and teaching effective parenting strategies, and has written for several professional publications, including *Family Therapy Networker*. She maintains a private practice in the Philadelphia area.